My JOURNEY *to the* LAND *of* MORE

LEONA CHOY

CHResources
P.O. Box 8290
Zanesville, OH 43702
740-450-1175

CHResources is a registered trademark of
The Coming Home Network International

Printed in the United States of America
14 13 12 11 10   1 2 3 4 5

ISBN 9780980006667

Library of Congress Cataloging-in-Publication Data

Choy, Leona F.
My journey to the land of more / Leona Choy.
    p. cm.
ISBN 978-0-9800066-6-7 (alk. paper)
1. Choy, Leona F. 2. Catholic converts--United States--
Biography. I. Title.

BX4668.C48A3 2010
248.2'42092--dc22
[B]

2010011667

Cover design & page layout by Jennifer Bitler www.doxologydesign.com

A TRIBUTE

I dedicate this story of my continuing spiritual journey, as well as all the books I have been privileged to write, *ad majorem Dei gloriam*, to the greater glory of God.

Seven years ago, I dedicated my autobiography and heritage saga, *Czeching My Roots*, to my godly Protestant paternal grandmother, Frantiska (Frances). She was my beloved live-in caregiver from my infancy. She quietly lived the Christian life before me and prayed that I would come to know God personally and embrace the Christian faith. Her prayers were answered from my first awareness of my Heavenly Father. Grandmother left this world nearly sixty years ago, but I believe she never stopped praying for my ongoing life in Christ.

One hundred and ten years ago and a quarter century before I was born, my young, paternal grandfather Jan (John) left this world before his fortieth birthday. Time and generations separated us, so of course I never had the joy of knowing him or climbing on his lap to hug his neck. In my search for my roots I was startled to discover that Grandfather was a passionately faith-filled Catholic man—*the only Catholic that I discovered in my ancestry!* Since prayers transcend space and time and their efficacy doesn't diminish, I believe there is a high probability that Grandfather Jan may have "prayed forward" through the years while on earth and has been "praying downward" from heaven for his descendants to be drawn by the Holy Spirit into the fullness of the Catholic faith. That would include *me*—one of his little granddaughters born in the following century on a different continent!

His loving prayers on my behalf would take eighty years from my birth to be answered: I was finally received into the one holy catholic and apostolic Church in 2005.

I dedicate this sequel to you, Grandfather Jan. I thought I had chronicled and completed my entire earthly journey in my original autobiography. Did you really pray this greatest of all surprises of spiritual abundance into my life? Thank you!

Between your continuing prayers and those of Grandmother Frantiska, which I believe are in full agreement now, I am rejoicing in the overflow of blessings in *The Land of MORE—the Catholic Church!*

CONTENTS

Acknowledgments

I bow my knee before God the Father, my Creator, Who by His grace and mercy chose me as His own in His sovereign plan before the foundation of the world.

I acknowledge Jesus Christ as my Savior and Lord of my life, as I have since childhood when I first became aware of His love and sacrifice for my salvation.

I bow in praise to the strong and tender ministry of the Holy Spirit whom Jesus promised would lead us into all truth.

Bless the Lord, O my soul, and all that is within me, for God's guiding hand upon my life from my conception.

I acknowledge with deep gratitude my biblical background in the Christian faith in the denominations and the non-denominational churches where I was led to accept and love Jesus Christ.

I am thankful for the inspired written Word of God that instructs me how to live pleasing to my Lord. I acknowledge the teaching Magisterium of the Catholic Church, the anointed authority of our Holy Father, Pope Benedict XVI, and Sacred Tradition passed on from Jesus through the apostles—all of which led me to the fullness of God's revealed Truth.

I am grateful for the authors of the stacks of books and tapes that helped pave the way for my latter journey of faith; for the ministry of EWTN (Eternal Word Television Network) lighting my way Home; for the guidance of the Coming Home

Network International and its helpful staff, especially for the encouragement of *The Journey Home* television program; for the patience and love of my longsuffering mentors Rod Bennett and Dr. Robin Maas who were my spiritual obstetricians; for the welcome and warmth and spiritual nurture of my home parish, Sacred Heart of Jesus Catholic Church in Winchester, Virginia; for our pastor Father Stanley Krempa and our faithful parochial vicars who continue to faithfully shepherd me; for my beloved new parish friends in abundance; for RCIA catechists Ed Norris and Paul Kielmeyer; and for my Confirmation sponsor, Jeff Zirkle.

I acknowledge the support of my four sons, Rick, Cliff, Gary, and Jeff and their families. They don't always understand their Mom but they love me, defend me, care for and encourage me, and trust God's work in my life.

I am thankful for the intercession on my behalf of the saints in God's presence and the prayers of my departed loved ones and friends—the "great cloud of witnesses" cheering me on to my Heavenly Home. We are united in the Communion of Saints.

I am indebted to the editorial expertise of Dr. Anita Gorman and the artistic talents of Jennifer Bitler for the cover design and to the staff of the Coming Home Network for the myriads of publishing details it takes to shape a manuscript into a book.

Leona Choy

FOREWORD

Rod Bennett, Author of *FOUR WITNESSES: The Early Church in Her Own Words*

I first met Leona Choy at the 2002 *Coming Home Network Deep in History Conference* in Columbus, Ohio. At that time she was immersed in painstaking research about the claims of the Catholic Church—but not with any intention to change her own strong evangelical orientation. She was out to militantly prove the Catholic claims unbiblical so she could "rescue" from error a close friend who had become Catholic.

God had other plans for Leona.

After several years of diligent, open-minded study and prayer, Leona herself was received into the Catholic Church just before her 80th birthday! I had the privilege of being one of her mentors on her "journey to the land of MORE," an unprecedented and unexpected faith paradigm shift for someone so advanced in years and so steeped in evangelicalism.

Leona grew up in midwestern America of immigrant parents from Czechoslovakia, with early classic Presbyterian roots. She read her way to a more lively faith as she devoured the works of evangelical giants and other Christian writers. Later in life Leona became the official biographer of Dr. Andrew Murray, the missionary statesman to South Africa so beloved of evangelicals everywhere.

From her teen years she offered herself for full-time Christian service and prepared for overseas mission work at

Wheaton College in Illinois—the Great Beating Heart of evangelicalism, as some would say. There she met her late husband, Ted, a committed Chinese-American Christian. They married after graduation and set off literally "on a slow boat to China." The spreading Communist revolution eventually made evangelization impossible inland and they continued to minister in Hong Kong and Singapore.

Some years later, God led the Choys to switch their focus to evangelizing Chinese students, professionals, and visiting scholars on North American campuses for the next 45 years.

Along the way, Leona helped to found an extensive gospel radio network, established a publishing company, and authored over 30 Christian books. She is the devoted mother of four adult sons, ten grandchildren, and six great-grandchildren.

Leona's daring spiritual journey can't be rationalized away or lightly dismissed. She was a fully seasoned, rock-solid pillar of evangelicalism, faithfully teaching God's Word, not a malcontent but happy in her faith and church. She was a veteran of over five sold-out decades of Protestant ministry.

Fully aware of the consequences, why and how could Leona risk making such a radical faith change so late in life? Her conversion to the Catholic Faith has to be explained step by step in her own words.

Let me encourage you to dig in!

INTRODUCTION

I have traveled extensively in America and abroad in my lifetime. When I set off on a journey, of course I knew my destination, and I purchased my plane ticket accordingly. When I drove, sometimes I requested an AAA TripTik® to map my route in detail. However, there are times when you aren't sure of your destination, especially if you are a passenger.

I was God's passenger on my recent, unexpected spiritual journey.

Only God knows what He planned for my life because He is both the Alpha and the Omega, the beginning and the ending. He knew me before I was formed in the womb, and He views my entire life from the panorama of eternity (Ephesians 1). He obviously included this late, surprising segment on my life route; He simply didn't tell me about it. Probably I would have reluctantly dug in my heels had He told me in advance.

Most of my life I was a contented passenger and confident that "Father knows best." I knew my ultimate destination since my early teens—I was headed toward Eternal Life in God's presence in Heaven. I would not attain it by my own merit; by faith I received the grace of God and through repentance, the forgiveness of my sins. My Savior Jesus Christ obtained it for me through His atoning death on the cross and His resurrection.

When I began this particular late-in-life spiritual journey, I was like Abraham in the Old Testament who, also in his advanced years, did not know where God was calling him. God had to blindfold me, so to speak, and position me on

His foreordained path. The journey I describe in this book was one I didn't plan and didn't want to take. Never would I have dreamed of such a wonderful unknown route to the same ultimate destination toward which I had been headed for a lifetime.

I was already in my late seventies. As a lifetime Christian, I figured that I knew most of what there was to know about the Christian faith and life. I am not a beginner; in fact, I am an "ender." I am chronologically challenged, as some say, since most of my life is behind me. I am a veteran Christian because I have had a personal relationship with Jesus since my youth. I have lived a full and satisfying life of learning, service, relationships, family, and a long career in Christian ministry. I had no complaint, no dissatisfaction; I was thankful to God for His lavish love and generous blessings. I have had a wonderful life!

I am the mother of four sons, grandmother of ten children, and a great-grandmother six times so far. I have a degree in Christian Education and taught the Christian faith in this country and overseas as a missionary. I was the wife of a minister for forty-six years. We cofounded a para-church mission organization and a Chinese church in our nation's capital. I have written and published many books, established a publishing company, and I am the president of a Christian radio station.

The reason for recounting the above is not to flaunt my accomplishments but to explain that with the writing and publication of my autobiography, *Czeching My Roots,* I thought I had pretty well wrapped things up. I didn't anticipate any surprising chapters in the rest of my life story, if God were to give me more bonus time on Planet Earth. I was being realistic. I didn't expect any Epilogue to my life that would differ markedly from the life I had already lived and the Protestant evangelical Christian beliefs I had firmly held for a lifetime.

In evangelical terminology, I considered myself born again, enjoying my assurance of eternal security, and convinced of *sola scriptura* and *sola fide*. I was a pre-tribulation dispensationalist; that is, I firmly believed in the imminent secret Rapture of the true Church as distinct from Jesus' Second Coming. Whatever was in the Bible I believed literally; anything that was not, I didn't feel obligated to believe. What further essential Christian truth could there be?

At the same time, from my youth God instilled a continual yearning in my heart for *more*, for a deeper, fuller, higher spiritual life. Without even thinking there might be prophetic implications in what I was writing, I titled the last chapter of my autobiography "Unfinished Symphony." I wrote, "I can't write the last chapter(s) of my life because I haven't lived them yet. I'm on tiptoe of anticipation to discover what gold God still has for me in my life treasure chest—how much *more* I can keep learning, how much closer to God I can come, and how much *more* fruit I can bear for Him...."

As a still fairly robust pilgrim, I want to "continue my pursuit toward the goal, the prize of God's upward calling, in Christ Jesus" (Philippians 3:14) until the end of my mortal life. I have always been and still am enthusiastic to follow God's truths that beckon beyond the horizon, to live on the cutting edge, to keep myself open to whatever experiences or life discoveries remain on God's agenda for my life. I am aware that *God's hand is still on my life.*

I agree with the saying, "Please be patient with me; God's not finished with me yet!" I want to "follow the Lord fully" as

Caleb in Old Testament days said he had done for a lifetime. When he was in his eighties, he asked for another mountain to conquer, a mountain that was promised to him forty years previously before his circuitous journey with the people of Israel in the desert.

Might there be another mountain for me? Was there still a *rest of the story?*

From my childhood I sensed that God had some special purpose for my life. I eagerly watched it unfold year by year and decade after decade, although I couldn't see the big picture. God is the Potter; I am the clay pot that He is molding. What did He have in mind for this insignificant, chubby, little Iowa-born child hiding shyly behind her Czech immigrant grandmother's apron? God kept working on the clay of my life, although I sometimes resisted. At times I tried to squirm out of His hand. Sometimes the clay of my life was marred or broken even while in His hands. As Jeremiah described in Chapter 18 of his book, if the clay was "spoiled in the Potter's hand, He remade it into another vessel, as it pleased the Potter." It is never too late; the clay is not ruined forever.

Using another metaphor, I wrote at the conclusion of my autobiography, "The Master Artist's painting on the canvas of my life must be nearly complete now. The picture He envisioned is taking shape. God is putting final touches on it—I am in 'finishing school.' How long will that process take? Only God knows. He is not in a hurry; God is eternal.

"I don't rule out that God might put some unexpected finishing touches on my painting late in my life. Was it not late in the wedding feast at Cana that Jesus turned water into wine? Wasn't the latter wine better than the wine served earlier? Didn't God make Anna and Simeon wait a long time in the

Temple until the final days of their lives before they saw the promised Messiah? Imagine the interminable wait of Abraham and Sarah and Elizabeth and Zachariah.

"God keeps coming up with surprises—more happy little things, bright color daubs as well as the darker strokes on my life canvas. After His brush applies them, it is obvious they enhance my painting; the new colors give dimension and depth. The picture would not have been complete without them."

What I wrote above may indeed have been prophetic. God seemed to be setting me up for some major changes ahead. Not only was He keeping me open, but keeping me alive—I have been a lung cancer surgery survivor for almost twenty years at this writing.

As I summarized my autobiography, I also compared my life to a jigsaw puzzle with thousands of pieces in the box. God deliberately kept me from seeing the finished picture on the lid. It takes a lifetime for the pieces of my life to fit together because many are small and some are look-alikes. If even one piece is missing, the puzzle is incomplete.

My puzzle will eventually be finished: "...the one [God] who began a good work in you will continue to complete it..." (Philippians 1:6). I won't see the finished picture until God Himself fits in the final perfect piece and I will view it in eternity. Then I will understand that every piece had its purpose and place. Without doubt I will see that under God's loving hand my life will have turned out just like the picture on His box!

Why should I have been surprised when God brought some wonderful late discoveries of *more* of His fullness into my life? I never want to refuse anything that comes from the Lord because *His hand is on my life* for my good and for His glory.

This book is an account of an earthshaking (to me) surprise

in the direction of my Christian life. It is the ongoing story of my soul, my own pilgrim's progress. The Holy Spirit draws each person onward in a unique way; I don't criticize anyone else's journey. I have tried to avoid generalizations about the entire evangelical context from which I came. I owe a great debt of appreciation to my Protestant heritage and the solid biblical foundation I received. My story is about how the Lord led me; therefore I speak only for myself.

This book is not a theological treatise, although my journey unfolded along a biblical route. I write with love and humility and vulnerability. I invite the reader to walk with me over the struggles and discoveries of my unexpected cobblestone road. I hope and pray that some of my readers may arrive happily together with me at the same destination.

An Attempt to
Define Terms

When I use the term "evangelical" I do not refer to a separate Protestant denomination. The term is somewhat ambiguous and is commonly used to describe a more conservative branch of any denomination or an individual within a denomination. It can also refer to someone in a nondenominational, independent ecclesial entity or to the entity itself. It is used at times to describe a para-church organization. There will likely still be disagreement no matter how we attempt to define the term.

Generally speaking, an evangelical Christian takes the Bible literally, considers himself "born again," and believes in *sola scriptura* (the Bible alone is our authority) and *sola fide* (we are saved by faith alone). The term "fundamentalist" denotes an even more conservative, often separatist, sometimes militant stance. The term "evangelical" may be used to describe a somewhat more tolerant attitude for divergent theological views and practices in contrast to "fundamentalist."

Some people refer to themselves by a vague term: "just plain Christians." They shun or even refuse all labels and maintain that simple faith in Jesus and the Bible is enough to identify a Christian. However, in time they too seem to divide and subdivide into separate groups based on individual or collective interpretations of the Bible. Before long, multitudes of new labels spring up and the "simple term" loses its original meaning.

Para-church organizations are Christian groups that usually

have a specific mission statement or method for evangelization of a certain segment of society or some special Christian project in their own country or abroad. They are not a church by definition. They are not usually officially associated with a particular church or denomination nor are they answerable to any ecclesial entity, although individual churches may participate in their mission.

All of the above would fit under the umbrella of Protestantism as distinct from Catholicism and the Orthodox churches. Protestantism had its origins in the 1500s as a protest against abuses in the Catholic Church, which admittedly needed reform and subsequently did reform itself. This resulted in the breakaway from the Catholic Church. Private interpretation of Scripture is a Protestant hallmark. The Protestant Reformation gave rise to the proliferation of denominations and groups based on the principle of individual interpretation of the Bible.

Because of the broadness of the term *evangelical* and the diversity of theological background of those who refer to themselves as such, it is almost impossible and inappropriate to make a generalization like "Evangelicals believe...." The fact is, they do not all believe alike. Moreover, evangelicals have no unified administrative authority to appeal to, no recognized continuing teaching body, and no uniform catechism by which to insure purity of doctrine, practice, discipline, or interpretation of Scripture. Evangelicals are usually noncreedal unless they are part of traditional denominations.

Therefore, in this book I have tried to be fair and genuinely appreciative of my strong biblical and spiritual background by saying, "As an evangelical I personally (thought, believed, practiced) such and such." I do not intend to paint all evangelicals with the same brush or speak for them. That would not be possible. Because this is my own story, I take responsibility only for my experience in my limited corner of the world.

The term *evangelical* is sometimes used interchangeably with *evangelistic*. *Evangelistic* more specifically refers to the desire and action toward leading another person to believe in Jesus Christ as Savior and Lord. As a Catholic, I continue to be *evangelistic*, to eagerly share the Good News of the Gospel with others.

Chapter 1

A LOOK IN THE
REARVIEW MIRROR

I was on my journey home from a successful seven-week speaking tour, a finale of sorts. I was promoting what was possibly my last book—my newly published autobiography, *Czeching My Roots*. After publishing thirty-some books and with my eightieth birthday not too distant, I thought perhaps it was time to retire.

Something unexpected happened on the way that became a catalyst to send me on another journey home in a direction I would never have imagined.

A Search for My Roots

Some of the books I have published were about the experiences my late husband Ted and I had during our lifetime of missionary witness among the Chinese people. Our service in China was primarily among the underground, persecuted Christians and among Chinese students and professionals on North American university campuses. Historical and contemporary biographies, including my husband's biography, help for fellow sufferers from cancer and other illnesses, other widows, and the writing craft were some of my themes. I established my own publishing company as an umbrella for some of my later works.

To wrap up my writing career I published the story of my

life. Having held workshops on autobiographical techniques, it was time to practice what I taught. After spending most of my adult life among the Chinese, my husband's people, I wanted to search for my own ancestral roots in Europe. My main purpose was, to paraphrase Psalm 102:19, "Let this be written for the generation to come that a people yet unborn may praise the Lord." I would never know future generations of my family, but they could know me through my writings. My life story would give me an opportunity to point the way to the Christian faith even to children not yet born. I hoped that my descendants would appreciate and be proud of the diversity of their ethnic, cultural, and religious roots.

I began to sense that God wanted me not only to leave a life legacy as a personal heritage saga but also to give a wider witness to God's faithfulness and guidance. With that in mind, my autobiography was a "Brag Book"—boasting on God and what He has done.

As I wrote, I gained a perspective on the entire scope of God's work in my life and explored the life and times of my ancestors and how that may have affected me. It was a fascinating look in the rearview mirror.

In hindsight, when I published my life story, I had no idea the book was only a launching pad for the rest of the story God still had in my future. My autobiography turned out not to be my final word after all; it would have an unexpected sequel to chronicle the surprising new chapters that would yet unfold.

After surviving life-threatening lung cancer and surgery in 1990 and attaining senior age status, I asked God, as I usually do at milestone times of my life, "Lord, do you have anything else planned for me before I leave this mortal life? I don't want to miss anything. I want it all!" I traveled several times to Europe on a treasure hunt to research my multiple roots. I spent precious weeks with Czech relatives whom I had newly discovered. I surprised myself by still being able to speak the Czech language I learned in childhood. I experienced daily life in the villages of my heritage as well as exploring magnificent Prague and historic castles in what is now the Czech Republic.

Besides my family and ethnic roots, I traced my religious roots as far back as I could—back to the Czech martyr-reformer Jan Hus born in 1372. I only researched my Protestant roots; I didn't realize at the time that there were any others. Although Hus was a professor at Prague University and remained a Catholic priest to his death, he is considered by Protestants as their champion and a major forerunner of the Protestant Reformation. He lived a full one hundred years before the reformers Martin Luther in Germany and John Calvin in Switzerland. He was burned at the stake for his attempted reforms against what I thought at the time was "the corrupt Roman papal Church." The reforms of Hus were not primarily theological; they were more along the lines of conducting Mass in the vernacular, his native Czech language, instead of Latin, and encouraging congregational singing. He also put great emphasis on the use of the Scriptures. The foregoing were among the heresy charges leading to his death.

As a result of the search for my heritage, I discovered that there was a "Faith of My Fathers, Holy Faith" in my bloodline, and I was an heir of that richness; I sensed a mandate to pass it on to my generation and generations to come. Surely the prayers of my godly ancestors have followed me. However, there were hidden dimensions of that faith that I did not discover until God led me to find an almost hidden taproot that I had completely overlooked.

I thought that our family's traditional faith was rooted in and limited to the Reformed tradition, the Moravian Church of the Brethren, whose roots led back to Jan Hus. Its origin was in the Moravia region of the Czech lands from which my ancestors came. In research for my book I made a pilgrimage to its beginnings in Herrnhut, Germany and explored my roots in the Pietistic movement of the 1700s in which Count Zinzendorf was instrumental. The Moravian Christians took turns every hour of the day and night for 100 years to pray for their missionaries in far-off lands. Their prayers launched the most extensive missionary movement in modern history. Out of that grew my heritage roots of the Evangelical Church of the Czech Brethren and the Czech Reformed Church, my immediate roots.

I never doubted that all my religious roots were Protestant, as were those of my late husband, Ted. It never occurred to me to check Christian history all the way back to the Early Church Fathers because that would have been Catholic history; I believed the Reformation was the important point of reference.

When I finished my autobiography, I didn't expect anything out of the ordinary to happen to me this late in life. With the apostle Paul I declared, "I have finished my course." I could never have imagined that I was on the verge of a positive faith upheaval in my life at an age when change of any kind is usually resisted, *status quo* is relished, and sitting in a rocking chair is considered more comfortable than rocking boats. I had no hint that God was getting me into position to enter a new and exciting season of my Christian life.

Heartland Beginnings

God arranged the props on the stage of my life when I was born. I was raised in the Heartland of America by first-generation immigrants from Czechoslovakia. I was the only child of loving parents who were good, moral people with a strong work ethic. However, their lifestyle did not include going to church. Sunday was their only day for rest and recreation. Nevertheless, they adamantly considered themselves Protestants.

In His life plan for me, God arranged that my paternal grandmother lived with us as my primary caregiver because both of my parents worked. A quiet, godly, simple Christian, she was a faithful worshiper at the little Czech Reformed Presbyterian Church in Cedar Rapids, Iowa where services were conducted entirely in the Czech language for the immigrants. Since Grandma Frantiska came to America late in life, she decided that it wouldn't be worthwhile for her to learn English. Her love, prayers, holy life, and living witness from my infancy led me to early Christian faith. Her spiritual influence has followed me all the days of my life, although she died when I was in my early teens.

Grandma saw to it that I was baptized as an infant in that little Czech church in my hometown. I did not understand until recent years that my baptism as an infant had been efficacious to wash away original sin, indwell me with the Holy Spirit, and mark me as a covenant child of God. When I became an evangelical Christian in my teens, I was taught that baptism was only for believers and should not be administered to infants. You became a Christian by saying wholeheartedly that you accept Jesus as your personal Savior. That was conversion; then you were saved. Baptism was not essential in the process since it was only a public symbol of an inner spiritual transaction that already had taken place.

My experience, however, seemed to trouble my evangelical friends because I could not point to the specific date of my conversion. From my earliest sense of self-awareness, I had a keen desire to seek and know God. "But you can't simply grow into being a Christian," I was told. "You must have a point of conversion to be saved." Nevertheless, I can't recall any time in my growing years that I ever deliberately rejected anything I had heard about God and Jesus and the Bible. I always eagerly sought for *more*. Far from perfect, my fleshly nature was strong, and I was quite a spoiled and self-willed child. At the same time, I hungered and thirsted after righteousness. True to His promise, God filled me with more faith and knowledge at whatever level I was able to understand spiritual matters.

The adults present at my baptism promised to "bring me up in the nurture and admonition of the Lord." They didn't follow through. Yet I never doubted that *God's hand was on my life* from before my birth, certainly from my baptism in the name of the Father, the Son, and the Holy Spirit. When I was given to God, He accepted that as a genuine gesture and began to unroll the scroll of His plan for my life.

During my early childhood, my best friend was Dot who lived across the street. She was from a Catholic family, never ate lunch meat on Friday, made the sign of the cross, and said her prayers kneeling by her bedside when we had sleepovers. I was impressed. But my parents never explained why they would never allow me to attend Mass when Dot invited me.

Nevertheless, God's hand was on my life. Seeds were planted.

I remember listening secretly and with great openness of heart to a Catholic priest on the radio (in the pre-TV era). I surreptitiously took a three-cent stamp from Daddy's desk (that was all it cost at the time to send a first-class letter) and wrote for a free crucifix as offered. I watched anxiously for the mail each day to head off my package secretly. When it arrived, I hid my precious treasure and took it out only in private in a secret corner of our attic where I knelt to compose original prayers to the God I didn't know yet. I lit a candle during my childish devotions; luckily I didn't set fire to the house. *God's hand was on my life.*

Other than Grandma and her godly example, no one in my extended family seemed interested in religion. When I was a toddler, she took me with her to the little Czech church. Although I understood little, I believe God's presence overshadowed me. Grandma taught me "Otce Nas," the Lord's Prayer, in the Czech language. Since I grew up without formal instruction in the Christian faith, I believe God Himself taught me. I gleaned basic theology from the words of Christmas carols; they truly contain the major teachings of the gospel. I took each morsel of truth into my young heart. From the carols I learned who Jesus was, why He came to earth, historical and biblical facts of His birth and life, God's salvation purpose, and what we should do to receive Him. I pondered those things in my young heart, but I was too shy to let grownups know that my thoughts were inclined toward God.

Dot invited me to a movie sponsored by her Catholic church titled *The Son of Man.* I conveniently neglected to tell my parents where it was to be shown, and they didn't suspect from the title that it might be religious. They allowed me to go with Dot, and by God's arrangement I was exposed for the first time to a depiction of the entire life of Christ in a black and white version of the gospel story. I was deeply moved.

An older neighbor child, June, took piano lessons; although

her family didn't attend church, she happened to have a hymnbook. She taught me to play the melody of "The Old Rugged Cross" with one finger. I was fascinated by the words and memorized all the verses. I eagerly accepted what Jesus' death and resurrection meant and how I should respond to His offer of forgiveness and salvation.

God's hand was on my life.

I lacked any formal Christian education until my early teens. The Christmas before the death of Grandma Frantiska, she gave Mother some money to buy an English Bible for me. Three-quarters of a century later I still have it. Perhaps Grandma also made Mother promise to bring me to church. Eventually Mother found a church in the Yellow Pages, Protestant of course, in the Reformed tradition. I found myself rather frequently sitting on the padded pews of the stately, historical First Presbyterian Church on a busy downtown corner.

There I was exposed to the reverence of the sanctuary, participated in a limited but beautiful liturgy, memorized the Apostles' Creed and the Lord's Prayer. We recited responsive readings from the Bible, and I learned the classic hymns of the faith. The elderly, robed minister preached rather scholarly sermons peppered with current events. I continued to eagerly accept for my spiritual nourishment whatever fragments of Christian truth I heard. I developed a serious, personal faith in God and in Jesus as my Savior. After going through an instruction class, I was confirmed at age thirteen to become a member of that Protestant church.

God's hand was on my life.

Not long after my confirmation and through the influence of Harriet, a Christian classmate in junior high, I transferred my membership to Westminster Presbyterian Church, which was considerably less formal and more forthrightly evangelical and evangelistic. The teaching in Sunday School and the preaching were soundly biblical, and I became well grounded in Scripture. The church had an enthusiastic youth group which enriched and protected my social life as a teen and deepened my spiritual life and personal commitment. Some of the friendships I formed there have been lifelong.

I climbed the typical evangelical ladder toward desiring God's best for my life. Even in my early youth, God's will became the focal point of my life. I loved Jesus with all my heart and soul and at age sixteen unreservedly surrendered my life to Him. I chose Romans 12:1-2 as my life verses. "I urge you therefore, brothers, by the mercies of God, to offer your bodies as a living sacrifice, holy and pleasing to God, your spiritual worship. Do not conform yourself to this age but be transformed by the renewal of your mind, that you may discern what is the will of God, what is good and pleasing and perfect." With other teens in our youth group I promised in the words of the old hymn, "I'll go where You want me to go, dear Lord, over mountains or plains or seas; I'll be what You want me to be...." This was my personal *fiat*; I was following Mary's example when she responded to the angel's message at the Annunciation. I too was allowing God to work out His sovereign plan for my future. *God's hand was on my life.*

I thought I had chosen God; in fact, God had chosen me in Christ before the foundation of the world...destined me...for His purpose according to Ephesians, Chapter 1.

Our church sponsored a fellowship group for teens called Life Work Recruits. We pledged that we were willing to go into full-time Christian service if God called us. Our energetic young pastor was born of missionary parents in China, so overseas missions were given a prominent place. The influences at that church led me to consider the foreign mission field as a career option. If we wanted God's best, our leaders told us, it meant becoming a foreign missionary.

I was serious about my commitment when I was eighteen, and I did not rescind it when I was eighty. I could not have imagined as a teenager what God would ask me to do, where He would lead me to go, what He wanted me to be during my long life. Nor what He would ask me to do in my later years. *God's hand was on my life.*

Even while I was in high school and later in college I wanted to move in deeper waters spiritually. I read many books about the Spirit-filled life and prayer written by men and women who lived in the centuries since the Reformation whom Protestants might call spiritual giants or saints. Included were the works of a prominent man of God to whose writings I was especially drawn. Dr. Andrew Murray lived in the late 1800s, and his books are eagerly read by succeeding generations of Christians worldwide who seek a closer, deeper, more intimate relationship with God. Little did I know that many years later I would connect with his descendants in South Africa for research, and I would become his authorized biographer. I contemporized and published a number of his books, as well as books by other deeper spiritual-life writers.

I considered myself a Protestant, although I had little knowledge of the historical or theological background for my position. I had no anti-Catholic antagonism; I was only vaguely aware that we were obviously "protesting against Catholics" whose beliefs were full of superstition. It was doubtful, I was told, whether Catholics were Christians. To be saved they would have to leave the Catholic Church where the pure gospel was obscured by idolatry, pagan ritual, and human tradition.

Climbing the Evangelical Ladder

Since I wanted God's best for my life, I continued to climb the typical evangelical ladder toward full-time Christian service. After high school I headed for conservative Christian (Protestant but not denominational) Wheaton College in Illinois and earned a degree in Christian Education. Although it was a liberal arts college, it was known as a citadel of evangelicalism and I received a solid biblical education.

It seems strange to me now, but the 1500-year gap between the Acts of the Apostles and the Reformation was a blank to me. I didn't elect to take any Church History courses since they were not required for my major. The important thing, I understood, was what the Bible said to me personally now and how I responded to the Great Commission to bring the gospel to the world. I was moved by the plight of people in other cultures overseas who were spiritually lost because no one had told them about God and the sacrifice of Jesus on the Cross. Missions became my passion; I believed God was calling me to full-time Christian ministry overseas.

The China Years

My future husband, Ted, was my classmate at Wheaton College. A third-generation Chinese Christian, he was educated in British Hong Kong. He came to the United States for his higher education, graduated from an evangelical seminary, and pursued further studies in the Bible at Wheaton. He took time out of his studies to serve in the U.S. Marine Corps and returned to graduate. Later he earned a graduate degree from the School of Religion at the University of Iowa.

We married in my Iowa hometown in 1947 and honeymooned "on a slow boat to China" with high hopes of investing our entire lives as missionaries for evangelism and church planting in China. However, it was just at the time when the rag-tag Communists rampaged victoriously over the political landscape in mainland China and forced all foreign missionaries, Protestant and Catholic, to make a swift exodus. Because we were blocked from working in inland China, we settled in British Hong Kong where my husband pastored a large Chinese church, and I helped train Chinese child evangelism workers. Later in Singapore my husband taught at a newly established theological seminary. The following several decades in missionary ministry with my husband were a high point of my service for the Lord among the Chinese people.

We were not able to go into China proper to engage in Christian work until some forty years later. Our mission work in the interim was to evangelize Chinese people elsewhere in Asia and in North America, especially the university student population. Eventually back in the United States with our three young sons in tow, one more born later, we founded a non-denominational Chinese Christian Church in the nation's capital. At the same time we co-founded a para-church university campus ministry for Chinese students and professionals which now extends across the United States and Canada. It is evangelical but not aligned with any denomination.

Ministry among Chinese people either in China or elsewhere in the world has little to do with denominationalism unless church-planting denominational foreign missionaries primarily from America impose it on them. Denominational relevance is limited to Europe and the Western world.

Fast-forwarding to the early 1980s, we were thrilled to be

able to enter China at last after diplomatic relations were re-established between China and the United States. For several years during that period I had the unique opportunity to conduct tours for groups of Americans to many of the famous historic and cultural sites in China which I had not previously seen myself. During the same decade, my husband and I also traveled extensively in a more or less clandestine ministry of encouragement and assistance to the persecuted underground Christians throughout China.

I can't communicate adequately what an immense spiritual privilege it was to have face-to-face and heart-to-heart encounters with people who were part of the suffering Church in China and to listen to their insider stories. Because Ted was Chinese, although an American citizen, he could freely travel anywhere and knew the major dialects of Chinese. I was able to caboose along to places where other foreign people did not have access.

What marvelous things the Holy Spirit had been doing in China for the fifty-plus years since the Communists sent all the missionaries packing! The Christians received the good seed of the Word from the missionaries, and the Holy Spirit remained in China to water and nourish the fledgling Chinese church! Statistics bear out that there have been more converts to Christ in China during the past few scores of years than in the entire world from the time of the early church until now! And more martyrs for the faith in China during that period as well.

My husband and I dressed down and traveled low profile so we would not draw attention and endanger our vulnerable Chinese Christian friends. They met for worship in clandestine family and neighborhood groups or out-of-the-way places at the risk of their lives. Those secret gatherings were the only

13

way for Christians to survive after the Chinese government confiscated their church buildings and imprisoned and killed thousands of pastors and church leaders. Christians were severely persecuted, sent to labor camps and prisons, and suffered indescribable torture. We worshiped with them in dirt-floor hideaways in remote villages and mountain hamlets, and in crowded urban areas where they and we were always on edge, due to the danger of police surveillance.

Those brothers and sisters in Christ told us awesome firsthand stories of courageous martyrdoms, inhuman treatment, extraordinary miracles, healings, and deliverances, some of which I recounted in several of my published books. To protect the identity of these stalwart, faithful Chinese believers, of whom the world is not worthy, I have ghostwritten a number of their biographies.

Through all these privileged spiritual adventures *God had His hand on my life.* And He saved some of the best wine until the last!

Chapter 2

CATAPULTED TOWARD A STRANGE ROAD

In 2002 God accelerated His plan to change my life. He was maneuvering my circumstances to prepare me for a faith paradigm shift that I would never have dreamed possible.

It happened like this. On my way home from the promotional tour for the release of my autobiography, I stopped for what I hoped would be a relaxing visit with a best-selling author friend (I'll call her Arlene). We always enjoyed intelligent and lively discussions about Reformed theology and our mutual Protestant beliefs. Arlene's husband had been a Presbyterian minister, and she was recently widowed.

As soon as we settled down for coffee, she bomb-shelled me with the news that she had become a Catholic! To say that I was stunned and speechless is an understatement. I thought she was out of her mind. What would cause her to fall into such serious heresy?

Why should her news upset me so much? During our mission work overseas, my husband and I were only incidentally aware of the Catholic Church in China and Hong Kong and other places in Asia. Although my husband studied in a Catholic high school for several years in Hong Kong, he was not influenced by that exposure because he was already well grounded in the Protestant faith,

The truth is, we knew next to nothing about Catholic

doctrine, and we didn't see any reason to investigate it. We were satisfied that in our biblical, evangelical faith we had the whole of God's revealed truth. I didn't think I was prejudiced; I was proud of being broadminded and tolerant. In the course of our ministry, my husband and I worshiped with and served happily together with many Christian denominations, independent churches, and para-church organizations in America and Asia. I wasn't militantly anti-Catholic, simply indifferent. I assumed that the Protestant Reformation had finally ushered in the true Church and put the Christian faith back on the right biblical track. I thought that the Reformation exposed the centuries of corruption in the Catholic Church and left it in the dust to wallow in its own errors. If Catholics persisted in worshipping Mary and dead saints, blindly followed papal authority, entangled themselves in tradition and superstition, engaged in pagan practices, and taught people to work for their salvation—well, that made them objects of our evangelization along with other cults. No one ever approached me to explain the authentic teachings of the Catholic Church.

Firing My Missiles

My immediate problem was what to do about my wayward friend. I took it upon myself to liberate Arlene from her mistake. My well-intentioned strategy was to point out all the biblical inaccuracies of Catholicism. Since both of us had a strong Protestant evangelical background, it was a level playing field. It never occurred to me that I could be on the wrong side of the truth.

I confronted Arlene: "Why in the world would you, in your happy retirement years, after you've spent all your life serving and teaching in the Reformed church, want to abandon true biblical theology? You are a seminary graduate, no less."

She answered, "I feel the real presence of Christ in the Eucharist."

How could she think that was an adequate reason to take such a drastic step?

"Arlene, you and I as Protestants know we have the presence of Christ with us all the time. Jesus lives in us in the person of the Holy Spirit. We don't have to go to a special place to experience the real presence of Christ. You shouldn't trust your feelings anyway. Isn't biblical doctrine enough to sustain your Reformed faith?"

"In the Eucharist the bread and the wine *become* the body and blood of Christ. He is there. I actually receive Christ— body, blood, soul and divinity," she explained.

Back at her: "You always believed, as I do, that the elements at the Lord's Supper are only symbolic. Come on, Arlene, you already "received Christ" when you were born again. That's once for all. You don't need to repeat it. Besides, a priest is only another human being. By what *hocus pocus* could he change the character of those material substances?"

I could see that I wasn't getting anywhere with Arlene. I tried another approach. "How about the rest of the Catholic trappings? Do you accept all that the Catholic Church teaches?" (I didn't really know what those other doctrines were, so I was smoke-screening my own ignorance.)

Arlene answered, "I really don't pay attention to the rest of the Catholic teachings. I'm only interested in the presence of Christ at the Mass."

That shocked me even more than her confession of becoming Catholic. "Weren't you required to go through some kind of indoctrination to join the Church?"

"Yes, but I only attended the classes because I was required to. I don't care about other Catholic doctrines."

I realized too late that I had probably offended her and hurt our friendship. In retrospect, it seems strange that I was more disappointed in her half-hearted commitment than in her heretical decision. I was sure she was making a terrible mistake by becoming a Catholic in the first place, so why should her lack of commitment to her false faith bother me? I believe it was because intellectual integrity and reason mean so much to me.

I backed off, but only temporarily, until I could gather my thoughts and confront her again. After all, Arlene was my long-time good friend, and I couldn't stand by and watch her make a tragic mistake that would surely affect her eternal destiny.

Because we live at a considerable distance from one another, I continued my drive home and took some time to assemble my ammunition. I sincerely hoped to help her out of her pitiful pit and restore a soul that had gone off track, as the Scripture says we should.

I did a little research about Catholic doctrines on the Internet in what I found later were primarily anti-Catholic web sites. Then I wrote Arlene a letter. As a writer, I tend to think more clearly when I can put my thoughts on paper.

My letter consisted of a long list of questions and declarations that I hoped would shock her into realizing that she had fallen into biblical error:

> "Arlene, I was right that you are required to believe everything Catholics teach in order to become one. You can't pick and choose; it is all or nothing at all.
>
> I found out that as a Catholic you have to believe in

an infallible Pope and accept whatever spin he puts on Scripture. You give up your precious Protestant privilege of interpreting the Bible on your own with the help of the Holy Spirit.

You have to accept what a bunch of cardinals and bishops decides you should believe. You check your intellect at the door of the Catholic Church.

Yes, I guess you do have to believe that the wine and bread actually change at the Mass and become the real flesh and blood of Jesus. But Jesus declared a lot of 'I Ams' in the gospels and we don't take those literally. They are metaphors.

Catholics trample *sola scriptura* underfoot. They don't believe that the Bible is our sole guide for faith and practice. They believe instead that the Catholic Church is the prime authority.

Catholics put equal faith in traditions and pagan superstitions which some early churchmen superimposed onto Holy Scripture. They even added extra books to the Bible. Jesus condemned traditions of men, don't you remember?

If you are Catholic, you have to believe that Peter was the rock on which Jesus built His church, and that he was the first pope. We know that it was Peter's confession that Jesus meant was the rock.

Catholics believe that the pope runs a visible, worldwide Church. We know that the real Church is invisible, consisting of all born-again believers.

The Catholic Church is like an exclusive club; they

don't allow other Christians to take Communion with them.

You have to worship all those statues and images. That violates the Ten Commandments about making 'graven images.' I found out on the Internet that you even have to worship relics—the bones and remains of saints!

Catholics pray for the dead and worship saints in heaven, even asking them for help like finding their car keys. All that is contrary to the Bible.

If you are Catholic, you're supposed to believe in the myth of Purgatory, that a Christian doesn't go directly to heaven when he dies. You have to be punished there for your sins even though Jesus forgave them.

Catholics have to do good works to earn their salvation. It is not by faith alone which you certainly know is clearly taught in the Bible.

In order to be Catholic, you have to believe that Mary was taken up to heaven in her body. And you have to believe she was sinless from the time she was conceived, and that she was a virgin all her life. No way—the Bible clearly mentions Jesus' brothers by name and his sisters.

Catholics pray to Mary instead of directly to Jesus. You can see how such overemphasis on Mary detracts from Jesus. God can't be pleased about that, can He?

You have to go to a priest, a mere man, to confess

your sins instead of doing what the Bible says—confessing directly to God.

Catholics call their priests 'Father' in spite of Jesus specifically telling us not to call any man Father.

You have to believe that the act of baptism saves you and takes away original sin. Being baptized is what Catholics call being born again. Wrong! Baptism is only a public symbol of what happens inwardly when you pray to accept Jesus into your heart.

Catholics have to endlessly repeat the Rosary in spite of Jesus' clear teaching against vain repetitions. Over and over they mumble those 'Hail Marys' as pagans do with their prayer wheels. Pagans use beads too.

Catholics believe in apparitions, the supposed appearances of Mary to people here and there around the world, and they build shrines to worship her.

Catholics still believe in the medieval hangovers of penance and indulgences that the Reformation rightly condemned.

Eternal security was always our important doctrine, Arlene. Once saved, always saved, no matter what. Catholics believe in eternal insecurity, that you never really know if you are saved until you arrive in heaven. Whatever happened to 'blessed assurance'?

As a Catholic you can't believe in the Bible teaching of the Rapture of the Church that we've discussed so many times together as our blessed hope.

Catholics don't believe Jesus will appear secretly at any moment to take true believers to heaven so they can escape all the troubles coming on our world.

Catholics need such fleshly trappings as bells and incense and candles and processions and bowing and kneeling and chanting in order to worship God. Those are just Old-Testament throwbacks not meant for New-Testament believers.

Dear Arlene, don't you feel embarrassed to call yourself a Catholic when you see the material excesses of the Vatican and all the pomp and ritual and lavish robes and extravagant architecture? How does that square with the simplicity of Jesus' lifestyle? I'm sure you know that the Vatican has a powerful influence on world politics. I read some shocking things on the Internet about the Pope being the antichrist; he will try to take over the world. The Catholic Church is the whore of Babylon of whom the Bible warns.

I hope you understand that it is only because I love you that I remind you of these things. I honestly can't bear to see you become part of such a corrupt and dangerous power structure. Even if you say you don't believe or even care about all the Catholic doctrines, you have nevertheless aligned yourself with the Catholic Church and you share in its heresy. It is guilt by association."

Well, I had discharged my arsenal, my litany of urban legends. It was no wonder that Arlene never answered my letter. I was a little uncomfortable that I might have overstepped our friendship bond because never again was she open to discuss any religious issues with me. Doing a fast-forward, I can hardly believe that I was so ignorant of the facts, that I so profoundly misunderstood the Catholic Church. How did I have the audacity even to speak of such matters? I have confessed my transgressions. "The man who pleads his case first seems to be in the right; then his opponent comes and puts him to the test" (Proverbs 18:17). Honestly, I wasn't acquainted with any Catholic at that time who could have set me straight.

Why did this matter continue to bother me? Why didn't I simply drop the subject? I could have maintained our friendship by avoiding further discussion of Catholicism. I could have chalked up the encounter with Arlene as just another small pothole in the road that shouldn't concern me. Why didn't I simply go on with my comfortable evangelical faith journey until the end of my life?

In hindsight, I see that *God's hand was on my life* in a way I could not have imagined. God was goading me out of my spiritual comfort zone. In fact, God might have been answering the prayers of an ancestor I never met, who lived long before I was born, someone who may have been praying for me from heaven to keep me moving forward on my journey Home.

Time for a Love Story...

I dedicated my autobiography to my beloved Protestant paternal grandmother, Frantiska, whose prayers and life witness helped to bring me into a personal relationship with Jesus Christ. I will be forever indebted to her.

Ah, but there was also a paternal grandfather, Frantiska's husband, whom I seemed to have overlooked in my quest for my heritage—my grandfather Jan (pronounced "Yahn"). In English his name is John. He is the only Catholic I know of on both sides of my family tree in previous generations. However, before Grandfather Jan there might have been a long lineage of Catholics—a spiritual bloodline and prayer line to which I am heir without being aware of it!

Prayers do not diminish or become diluted with the passage of centuries, nor are they relegated by God to some dusty heavenly filing cabinet. He does not overlook them because the prayers are too impossible or too trivial. Prayers are recorded in God's eternal memory and never go unanswered because God is eternal; the past and present and future are all as present to Him.

I know it to be true that both my paternal grandmother and my husband's paternal grandmother *prayed forward* for "the generations yet to be born"—for the spiritual conversion of their progeny. That is why I believe my grandmother Frantiska's prayers during her lifetime, and even now as she intercedes for me from the Father's House, as Jesus called Heaven, are still efficacious for me. They are as powerful now as they were when she was on earth caring for her chubby, shy little granddaughter—me.

Let me tell you a love story that may be relevant to why I was drawn by the Holy Spirit to explore a faith paradigm shift even on the verge of my eightieth year.

I find it difficult to visualize my grandmother as she was during her youth since I knew her only in her old age. What was she like as a young bride, and even before that, as a late teen in the mid-1880s, a girl who fell in love with a handsome young soldier just returned from the Austrian wars?

That scenario took place in the little village of Radlice

(Rahd-lee-tseh) in the province of Moravia in what is now the Czech Republic. Obviously Jan must have been likewise smitten with the lovely Frantiska because he dared to propose a marriage that would thrust them into the forefront of a religious controversy. Unfortunately, bitter religious wars were waged between Protestants and Catholics in that century; the ramifications affected everyone in the tiny village in which my ancestors lived.

What was the problem that seemed insurmountable? Frantiska was a devout evangelical Reformed Protestant girl, and Jan was an equally strong, faithful, and uncompromising Catholic!

Love obviously conquered differences and the young couple braved the seeming impossibilities and scandal, ignored the displeasure and opposition of their families and neighbors, and married. I don't know in which church the sacrament took place, but my guess is that it was the Catholic Church.

One major decision they faced was in which faith they would agree to bring up the children they expected to have. I did learn from the recollections of certain elderly relatives that the young couple solved the problem with a sort of pre-nuptial agreement—whether official or unofficial is not known. Jan would have the boys born to them baptized Catholic, and Frantiska could take the girls with her to the Protestant church. I was surprised to learn from my relatives that my father Frantisek (Francis or Frank) was one of the four sons baptized Catholic. I have the original copy of his baptismal certificate, which was the sole document from which I was able to gain information and begin research on my family roots.

The agreement apparently worked for them since they enjoyed a happy and harmonious marriage despite the fact that on Sunday mornings the family separated at the door. Grandfather set off on foot with his four sons through the deep forest and over the hills to Mass at the Catholic church. Grandmother, with their two daughters in tow, took a different route to the Evangelical Reformed church in Velka Lhota.

Unfortunately, Grandfather Jan died before the age of forty from breathing the stone dust in the environment of his job as a stonemason. From that time, Grandmother took all six children to the Protestant church. Eventually the entire family, one by one, immigrated to America and settled in Iowa. To my knowledge, when the children reached adulthood, none of them seemed inclined to practice serious religious faith or to raise their children in any church. Ancestral prayers are efficacious, however! A few of my close relatives did come to (Protestant) faith in their later years, including my father. In the following two or three or four generations, quite a number of my cousins have become Christians, some even Catholics. The Holy Spirit continues to draw our extended family to Jesus Christ. The faith of our fathers is living still!

God's hand was on MY life as He drew me into His Family early in childhood. The prayers of my ancestors, and my husband's ancestors, together with our own prayers, continue to be answered in the generations of our children, our children's children, our great-grandchildren, and will be in those yet unborn.

Although Grandfather Jan died more than a quarter century before I was born, his prayers may be a key to my becoming Catholic. He may have been interceding for me for over 100 years in the presence of God: *"Lord, bring my little granddaughter HOME into the one, holy, catholic, and apostolic church!"*

I dedicate this sequel book, the "rest of the story" beyond my original autobiography, to Grandfather Jan.

Preparing for a Dramatic Rescue!

Back to my journey—I believed that my evangelical faith was unshakable because I assumed that biblical truth was clearly on my side. I didn't need to review my own position; I knew it well.

To maintain my personal integrity, however, I felt that I should honestly examine Catholic doctrines firsthand, not from hearsay, so I could discredit their fallacies and delusions. I would prepare myself "to be ready to give an answer to anyone about the hope that was within me." That should not really be difficult. I thought of myself as God's "rescue squad" and expected a no-contest victory to reclaim my wandering friend, Arlene, from her heresy. I had no doubt that after a lifetime in the Protestant camp, I was well qualified to shoot holes in two thousand years of Catholic faith and practice. (What presumption!)

At the Crossroads

On a positive note, my heart was tenderly inclined toward the Lord. I was sure that God would not fail to guide me in this situation, as always, because He and I have a long track record.

I sincerely prayed, "Lord, please don't let me be shaken. As an aging, experienced sheep, I am not a novice in recognizing my Shepherd's voice. I'm setting off on an unfamiliar road, so I plead as Moses did, 'Lord, if You do not go with me, I will not go.' Only with the confidence of Your presence and guidance, will I proceed.

"God, You are Truth; protect me from falsehood. Keep me from taking the wrong path and making foolish mistakes at this late season of my life. Many people look to me to demonstrate steady faith. Don't let me slip from Your hands. You have been working on my clay pot for such a long time; keep me from ruining the clay by falling into error. Lead me not into temptation but deliver me from evil and guide me in the way of Life Eternal."

I was sure that the Lord would answer my heartfelt prayer.

I leaned heavily on Scriptures that affirmed my desire to test and reflect on the truth. "Examine yourselves to see whether you are living in faith; test yourselves..." (2 Corinthians 13:5). "Beloved, do not trust every spirit, but test the spirits to see whether they belong to God, because many false prophets have gone out into the world.... This is how we know the spirit of truth and the spirit of deceit" (1 John 4:1 and 6). "Test everything; retain what is good" (1 Thessalonians 5:21).

This was where I stood: I have trusted God since the Holy Spirit drew me into a personal relationship with Jesus Christ in my early teens. My desire as long as I can remember has been to try my best to listen to and obey the leading of the Holy Spirit.

Throughout my life I have prayed a daily morning prayer to offer myself to God, acknowledging His Lordship over my life in detail and surrendering myself entirely to His will. I expressed it in different ways through the decades as I matured, but in essence it is as follows:

MY COMMITMENT. Jesus Christ, You are Lord of my life. I acknowledge You to reign as King with full authority over my body, soul, spirit, mind, emotions, and will. Rule over all that I am, all that I have, and all that You have given me. I affirm Your Lordship over every relationship, responsibility, appetite, and ambition.

"I urge you, therefore, brothers, by the mercies of God, to

offer your bodies as a living sacrifice, holy and pleasing to God, your spiritual worship" (Romans 12:1).

TRANSFORM ME. Continue this day to shape me into Your image through whatever circumstances You choose to bring into my life. Mold me until You finish the work in and through me that You destined from before the foundation of the world.

"All of us, gazing with unveiled face on the glory of the Lord, are being transformed into the same image from glory to glory, as from the Lord who is the Spirit" (2 Corinthians 3:18).

LIVE THROUGH ME. Jesus, You already live in me by Your indwelling Holy Spirit. Help me express Your life as I walk in the Spirit. May I not respond according to the flesh either to adversity or prosperity.

"I say, then: live by the Spirit, and you will certainly not gratify the desire of the flesh" (Galatians 5:16).

I DESIRE TO GLORIFY YOU. I long to be a clean, pure, and holy vessel to glorify You as I carry within me the treasure of Your presence and the fullness of Your power. I want to keep myself open to the continuous filling of Your Holy Spirit. I want to bear more fruit to please You and use whatever gifts of the Spirit You give me to help build Your Kingdom.

"But we hold this treasure in earthen vessels, that the surpassing power may be of God and not from us" (2 Corinthians 4:7).

SCHEDULE FOR ME. This day bring into my life everything and only whatever and whomever You desire—in person, by letter, e-mail, phone call, thought, impression, prayer, event, or circumstance. Help me to be aware that interruptions and changes are not accidental or incidental but are my opportunities and Your appointments meant for Your glory and for my good.

"We know that all things work for good for those who love God, who are called according to His purpose" (Romans 8:28).

GRANT ME DISCERNMENT. Show me Your priorities for the hours of this day. As I follow Your guidance, give me Your strength and wisdom to accomplish the tasks that You've specifically appointed for me. I want to hear Your voice clearly and then obey and follow You fully. May I be careful to abide in You and maintain my "first-love" relationship with You. While I do with love the good works You have commanded, may they not deter me from a close walk with You.

"Martha [was] burdened with much serving... anxious and worried about many things... The Lord said, there is need of only one thing..." (Luke 10:40-42).

As I began my exploration in an unknown direction, I relied on God's promise in Philippians 1:6, "I am confident of this, that the one who began a good work in you will continue to complete it until the day of Christ Jesus." Wherever I was headed, I knew God would not overlook my honest commitment to His will. I counted on God to keep me from being deceived.

Nevertheless, at this crossroads I wondered why God was veiling the journey ahead of me and keeping me in suspense. Would I be reluctant to go on if I knew where He was really leading me? Would I dig in my heels and kick and scream? Probably! It is likely God wanted me to keep trusting Him totally without seeing where the road ahead was leading.

I would go on because I knew *God's hand was on my life.*

Chapter 3

Stumbling Over the Cobblestones

Sizing Up the Road

I visualized the composition of the Christian road on which I traveled all my life as being paved with cobblestones. Most, but not all, of the stones were joined smoothly together and had familiar labels: gospel, prayer, salvation, preaching, witnessing, faith, Trinity, Bible study, church, Jesus Christ, incarnation, virgin birth, worship, grace, heaven, hell, cross, missions, resurrection, redemption, assurance, and service. These were the settled lifetime infrastructures of my evangelical world.

So were love, joy, peace, mercy, spiritual fruit, spiritual gifts, the second coming of Christ, angels, holiness, Baptism, the Lord's Supper, miracles, and forgiveness.

Neatly fitting in were the Ten Commandments, creation, healing, marriage, family, blessing, morality, truth, conscience, right to life, hope, prophecy, millennium, and the Rapture.

However, two large stones on the roadway—*sola scriptura* and *sola fide*—seemed a little loose. Never mind; I was sure I could cement them in place. So far, so good. I walked steadily and joyfully for a lifetime along this familiar faith-thoroughfare.

On closer scrutiny, I noticed gaps that I had not previously seen among some of the familiar cobblestones. Other stones, some large as boulders and some small as pebbles, seemed to

31

be out of place and lying on top of or beside the familiar stones of my evangelical faith. Their labels seemed strange. I detected them when I started to research the Catholic faith. My first thought was to toss them aside as unnecessary. I couldn't imagine how they might fill the gaps among the familiar stones to make a smoother surface. Why, they weren't even words that I found in the Bible.

Some of the labels on the uncommon stones were Sacred Tradition, Real Presence, creeds, priests, Deposit of Faith, liturgy, Mass, Assumption, Mediatrix, veneration, hierarchy, apostolate, Magisterium, Pope, and infallibility.

And more: Vatican, Purgatory, Marian doctrines, Eucharist, genuflection, confession, sacraments, sacramentals, host, celibacy, merit, stigmata, relics, mysteries, catechesis, apparitions, homily, religious orders, and icons. Still more: crucifix, shrines, beatific vision, transubstantiation, rosary, indulgences, novenas, suffering, Church Fathers, reparation, expiation, and intention. More yet! Encyclical, scapular, hypostatic union, monstrance, cenacle, absolution, and chrism.

What a pile of unfamiliars! What language was this?

Since Jesus called Himself The Way, I sincerely asked Him, "Guide me…make straight Your way before me" (Psalm 5:8). Other translations offer expanded meanings: "straight" implies not crooked; "level" means not up and down, rough, or with potholes; "plain" is forthright, not confusing; "clear" implies in focus and pure. That was the kind of road I was accustomed to—a smooth one without obstacles. I didn't realize that God planned for some of the unfamiliar stones to act as speed bumps. He wanted me to slow down and consider them more seriously, but how could I deal with so many?

Since there is no darkness in God, only light, I counted on

Him to shine His light on my path and reveal both truth and error. No, I would not turn back with fear of the unknown or because I refused to leave my faith comfort zone.

God's hand had always been on my life for good.

Setting Off

I imagined a directional signpost at the side of the road. It read, *To Search for the Truth.* "Yes, that's my plan. At the same time, I asked myself, "Why do I need to search for truth? I've already found God's truth and lived it for a lifetime; I only need to defend it." Of course, I always pursued MORE truth from the time I first sought God. Jesus said He was sending His Holy Spirit "to lead us into all truth." Was it possible that there was MORE truth beyond what I knew? I had this going for me: I honestly determined to keep an open mind.

"From the Horse's Mouth"

I was looking for unvarnished truth. I wanted to be without prejudice and objective, and maintain a cool, clear head. Jesus taught me to treat people fairly, not to jump to a hasty conclusion. "Be quick to hear, slow to speak..." (James 1:19). I didn't think I'd receive authentic answers from the average lay Catholic who might not even be sure of what his Church teaches. Nor could I measure my conclusions against how some Catholics imperfectly practice their faith. I could easily round up plenty of poor examples among Protestants, too, since there are an endless variety of interpretations of Scripture. Before long I also discarded the obviously biased anti-Catholic web sites that were loaded with misinformed rhetoric. Unfortunately, I had relied on those to shape my initial comments to Arlene. I regretted that. "Love is never rude...our knowledge is imperfect..." (1 Corinthians 13:5, 9).

Where would I find the truth? I would have to go directly to authentic Catholic sources for the core of their teaching. I'd search the Internet, go to the library, check the bookstores, and observe the Catholic Mass firsthand. The latter would be scary. I wasn't ready for that yet.

On my Internet search I discovered more than a dozen web sites loaded with user-friendly reliable Catholic sources and interactive Q & A. I spent hours and days perusing them. This was new for me; I had never invested serious time to understand that faith.

Surfing the TV one day, I came across the Catholic channel, EWTN, the *Eternal Word Television Network*. I had no idea there was such a thing. I became a frequent but skeptical viewer. I was especially intrigued by the weekly *Journey Home* program which aired conversion interviews with prominent people, even clergy from a variety of denominations, who had been non-Catholic or anti-Catholic. Supposedly they "found their way home" to the Catholic Church. I shook my head at such a possibility. I concluded that such Protestants must not have been well grounded in the Bible. I heard quite often of Catholics who defected and "found Jesus" and became evangelicals; is it possible that there is a reverse flow? Curiosity kept me watching.

I ordered more than a dozen books and many audio tapes and CDs from EWTN. I expected to spot their errors and thus reinforce my Protestant position. My thorough investigation took several years.

I spent time in two "closets." I was on a private, hidden, and largely undisclosed journey. I am not usually secretive, but I didn't want to needlessly rock any boats. I stayed "in the closet" researching clandestinely. I logged hundreds of hours reading, viewing, listening, taking notes, and comparing Catholic doctrine with the Scriptures. I ordered more Catholic books. The trail I was following was so foreign to my evangelical thinking. I read slowly because the vocabulary was strange; theological words to which I was accustomed did not seem to have the same meaning.

I also spent time "in the closet" of prayer pondering all these things in my heart and asking God to help me sort them out. I recorded the details of my journey in a notebook so I could monitor my progress. *God had His hand on my life.*

I asked a Catholic friend to buy a Catechism for me. If I shopped for one myself, I might have brought it home in a brown paper sack. She delivered the bulky, unabridged *Catechism of the Catholic Church.* That turned out to be my primary source—an authoritative summary of official teaching on every one of my questions by topic with plenty of biblical references. I knew of nothing to compare with that in the Protestant world because there is no uniform, agreed-upon system of catechesis and biblical interpretation.

Nearly every week I tuned in to EWTN for a full hour of systematic teaching by Father John Corapi on Catechism topics; I followed along in my copy by paragraph numbers. I marked it heavily with a yellow highlighter. I was ready to pounce on anything contrary to Scripture. What a surprise that Father Corapi used the Bible as underpinning for every teaching, and the Catechism did likewise!

On EWTN I was amazed to hear excellent biblically-based sermons. Catholics affirmed the inspiration of the Bible and, contrary to what I had been told, Catholic leadership strongly encouraged personal and group lay Bible study.

The Bible expositions of Dr. Scott Hahn, whose denominational Protestant background was similar to mine, intrigued me. I did not feel threatened when I listened to his enthusiastic presentations because his logic and exegesis were sound, and he was clearly a Bible scholar of high caliber. He shed new light on doctrines that were familiar to me but obviously had fuller ramifications than I had ever realized. I didn't feel I was being brainwashed; I simply opened myself to a broader biblical outlook. I ordered a stack of his books and tapes so I could delve more thoroughly into specific topics. I kept waiting to find the errors which I was certain would come to light. However, I couldn't find any loopholes in Scott's Bible expositions.

Making Progress

As time went on, along that cobblestone road I noticed a new imaginary signpost. It had now become "*To Better Understand Truth.*" A slight correction but still in line with my desire. Nevertheless, I reminded myself, "You are simply an investigative reporter trying to be objective and intellectually honest about an opposing theological framework." The whole thing was my friend Arlene's problem, I told myself; it was not my problem. I should be objective; therefore, I would keep my findings at arm's length.

However, I began to sense a personal identity crisis. When I started on my journey, I seemed to be wearing an imaginary placard on my back that read "*Protestant.*" As I proceeded along the road, I noticed that label must have dropped off somewhere. I realized I was no longer protesting anything or anyone. I had worn such a designation in ignorance. So I substituted the placard "*Evangelical.*" That seemed to be broader, at the same time more focused, and raised fewer red flags. A little farther along the exploration road I reached around my shoulder to check on the placard again. It had somehow been altered to read simply "*Christian.*" Well, I could accept that as a more comfortable and authentic fit. Little did I know that there were a few more identity changes down the road.

Digging to the Foundations

I began my research by zeroing in on the largest unfamiliar boulders on the cobblestone roadway. Smaller strange stones were clustered around each large one. I figured that if I could take care of the big boulders one at a time, I could dispense with the cluster of smaller stones around it, and my path would be considerably smoother.

Several of the most prominent boulders were *Authority, Sacraments, and Saints.* Most of the smaller stones were clustered around those. I would start with Authority, since so many of my questions hinged on that. The cluster around it included "one holy catholic and apostolic Church" (in the words of the Nicene Creed), tradition, hierarchy, Magisterium, the Papacy, infallibility, Vatican, Deposit of Faith, and Church Fathers. Refuting this big boulder seemed to be my top priority.

I started my study as near in time to the life of Christ and His apostles as I could. This was a significant era in history that I knew almost nothing about—the Early Church Fathers, the immediate successors of the apostles. It never before seemed important to pay attention to those historical figures because my Protestant faith was rooted in the Reformation occurring in the 1500s. After all, wasn't that when the full truth of justification by faith alone, *sola fide,* finally came to light after the prolonged corruption of the gospel by Catholics for fifteen centuries? *Sola scriptura,* the authority of the Bible alone, replaced the false authority of the Papacy and the Magisterium, the hierarchy of the Catholic Church. Didn't the Reformation usher in authentic freedom with its emphasis on private interpretation of Scripture?

The facts as I perceived them were that because of certain papal abuses and widespread Church corruption the former Catholic priest, Martin Luther, saw the truth clearly at last and launched the Protestant movement. The fallout from this breakthrough or rather breakup was, regrettably, that many denominations and sects and groups proliferated, fragmented, divided, and subdivided. Any difference in the interpretation of something in Scripture, however slight, seemed to give rise to another splinter group. To this day there is no end in sight of the divisions. Was Jesus' prayer "that they may be one" answered more perfectly through the Protestant movement? I began to take a new, hard look at the roots and results of the Reformation.

The Whole Truth and Nothing but the Truth?

My reading and study of the Early Church Fathers opened my eyes. The divine strategy Jesus initiated by establishing His Church actually worked well right from the beginning. What He intended did happen after He gave authority to Peter and His apostles to lead the Church that He Himself declared He would build. John recorded Jesus saying in John 16:12-14, "I have *much more* to tell you, but you cannot bear it now. When he comes, however, being the Spirit of truth he will guide you to *all truth*. He will not speak on his own, but will speak only what he hears, and will announce to you the things to come. In doing this he will give glory to me, because he will have received from me what he will announce to you."

How else could I interpret those plain statements? I had never before read them in the context of history. Jesus' promise was specifically to His apostles! It was obviously upon *their* minds that the Holy Spirit was acting to give them perfect recall and understanding. With their deaths God's divine revelation ceased. From then on it was a matter of faithfully and meticulously passing on that completed revelation and unpacking its meaning and implications through the ages to come. What we read in the Catechism is not a source of new revelation.

Some stable, enduring authority structure was needed to safeguard its purity. It was for this reason that Jesus established His visible Church. The Holy Spirit would hover over the Church to preserve and protect the fullness of that revelation. Obviously there was MORE that Jesus taught his apostles and which He wanted succeeding generations of His followers to know—MORE that God wanted me to learn, too. Of course it required a visible, united Church authorized by Jesus Himself to pass it on!

I don't know why it had never registered with me before, but it began to be so clear to me now: there is MORE precious truth that Jesus taught and things He did that are not in the bound book, the Bible I hold in my hand! What right do we have to close the door of access to that truth since it is available?

The apostle John in his gospel (20:30-31) wrote, "Jesus performed *many other signs* as well—signs not recorded here— in the presence of His disciples. [John knew; he was there!] But these have been recorded to help you believe...." In the last two verses of his gospel John repeated, "There are still *many other things* that Jesus did, yet if they were written about in detail, I doubt there would be room enough in the entire world to hold the books to record them." The gospel writers were purposely selective under the Holy Spirit's promised oversight. That is what imparted to the writings the value of inspiration.

I had to admit how logical it was that *only part* of the full teaching of Christ was put in writing, doubtless a very small part given the three-year period of His public ministry. Up to that point it was all transmitted orally by preaching and teaching. It is doubtful that the apostles distributed handouts with their sermons or that the audience was taking notes. Certainly there were no recording devices. There was far MORE that the apostles knew and taught their converts; it was also important, and of course they eagerly conveyed it. Why would we not want to know as much of it as possible? Why would *I* not find it imperative to know? I spent much time unpacking this insight because it was so critical to my expanded understanding.

Paul and the other writers of the pastoral letters never claimed to include all the truth there was to convey. In the main they wrote letters to answer certain questions or problems that arose. Or they addressed aberrations of truth that had arisen, corrected false teaching, or combated heresy. It made sense that they took for granted what was commonly known and practiced by most early Christians; they did not need to repeat that in every letter. In Acts 2:40 we read about Peter, "In support of his testimony he used *many other arguments....*" Obviously, his entire sermon wasn't recorded for us. We don't have all those *other words.* Nevertheless, the apostles must have taught regularly and clearly from those *many other things* they had "... heard...seen...looked upon...touched...of the word of life..." (1 John 1:1-3). That was what was faithfully passed on in the Early Church and guarded for accuracy by the Holy Spirit.

I was in unfamiliar territory! I was trying to tread water and stay afloat in strange non-Protestant waters—or so I thought.

Tradition—tradition

I discovered that "tradition" was not really the dirty word I had always supposed. The kind of tradition that Jesus condemned in the gospel account was something specific that arose in his times and culture—the endless, superimposed, legalistic interpretations and rules that the Scribes and Pharisees appended to the Mosaic Law. There is good tradition, what the Catholics call "Sacred Tradition" with a capital "T" as opposed to man's tradition with a small "t" which is more like custom. In 1 Corinthians 11:2 Paul clearly wrote, "I praise you because you always remember me and are *holding fast to the traditions* just as I handed them on to you." He reinforced this thought in 2 Thessalonians 2:15, "Therefore, brothers, stand firm. *Hold fast to the traditions* you received from us, either by word or by letter." And in the next chapter (3:6), "We command you, brothers, in the name of the Lord Jesus Christ, to avoid any brother who wanders from the straight path and does not follow *the tradition you received from us.*" How is it possible that I overlooked those verses for so long?

Paul himself, not having known Jesus in person, was a receiver of those Sacred Traditions passed on to him. Timothy, too, was a link in the chain. It now made sense why Paul admonished Timothy in his letter (2 Timothy 2:2): "The things which you have *heard* from me through many witnesses you must *hand on to trustworthy men* who will be able to teach others." This entrusting, this passing on of the apostles' oral teachings, is the content of what the Catholic Church calls "Sacred Tradition." It is MORE than Scripture, but it never contradicts Scripture.

The inspiration of the Bible does not change nor does the composition and authority of the canon of Sacred Scripture. The richness and authenticity of Sacred Tradition should not be overlooked either—a significant, startling new thought to me!

I did not realize that the Early Church Fathers wrote a great volume of literature from which we can learn, and that it is preserved and accessible. For the first time, I became acquainted with the writings of Clement of Rome, Ignatius of Antioch, Justin Martyr, and Irenaeus of Lyons. They are important because they lived the closest to the time of the apostles; they are the early recipients of the Sacred Tradition. My studies soon extended to Cyprian, Origen, Polycarp, Ambrose, Augustine, and others.

These men and their writings were not inspired in the sense that the Holy Scriptures are, nor were their writings entirely without error. They did not claim inerrancy or new revelation. God's revelation was completed with Jesus and the apostles. Their insights and faithful examples, however, are helpful to our spiritual lives. In the young Church, some did not grasp apostolic teachings perfectly and heresies arose; moreover, communication with established leadership at a distance was primitive. Nevertheless, we have more than just an authentic glimpse into how the Early Church conducted its worship and what the first Christians believed and taught and practiced. We can also know to whom they looked for leadership. "Inquiring minds want to know" because it is important.

The Early Church was still in the afterglow of Jesus' life and death and resurrection and just beginning to apply the truths and pass them on. There would continue to be a normal and legitimate development of doctrine, an unpacking of the meaning of the truths once delivered which continues to the present day. Revelation and doctrine do not change; our fuller understanding of them grows. For instance, the Catholic Catechism is not considered a source of new revelation; rather it is a systematic presentation of divine revelation. The implications continue to be applied to new situations throughout all generations. I found myself in theological shock!

Pillars Switching, Supports Crumbling

I was taught and took for granted that the Bible alone was the pillar and support of God's truth. I never questioned that premise. I was sure that was what the Bible claimed for itself until I looked up 1 Timothy 3:15 and read, "...God's household, the *church* of the living God, the pillar and bulwark of truth...." My major superstructure of *sola scriptura* was crumbling! To be intellectually honest, I had to acknowledge the importance of those oral traditions passed on to the Church and by the Church. Could it really be true that the Church which Jesus established was concrete, discernible to the senses, and not solely an invisible entity?

When I followed the scriptural trail, I found that the Bible actually does not support *sola scriptura*; nor does it claim that for itself. It took me a while to regain my balance after that earthquake. I couldn't easily accept such a paradigm theological shift. If *sola scriptura* were to collapse, would some other basic Reformation principles also topple like a row of dominos? Rather than cementing the large, loose rock of *sola scriptura* firmly back into the roadway, would I have to remove it?

A Challenge to My Integrity

I looked anxiously toward the side of the road—I was afraid that the signpost had changed again. I was right! I saw an arrow pointing forward, and it read, "*To Acknowledge The Truth.*" That was a major switch, a disturbing change of focus! Just where was this road leading? Could I still turn back? Could I really keep my conclusions at arm's length so they would not disturb the comfort zone of my own life and faith?

Climbing among the Branches

I was not looking for some novel truth. I kept assuring myself that I had already found the once-for-all revealed Truth of God early in my life in the written Word of God. I had a personal relationship with the Word made flesh, Jesus, my Savior who declared, "I AM THE TRUTH." I had accepted Him as Lord of my life, had loved Him for as long as I could remember, had been trained in scriptural Truth, walked in it, delighted in it, and taught it for a lifetime to others who were seeking it. I continue to do so.

Ultimate Truth is unchangeable, yet it is not stagnant. Throughout my life I continue to find new insights and nuances of God's Truth—but they remain a part of God's Ultimate Truth. I worshiped in, had fellowship with, and served happily in denominational Protestant churches as well as in nondenominational Bible churches, community churches, charismatic gatherings, indigenous churches in the mission field, para-church ministries and movements, cross-cultural churches, ethnic churches, and other types of Christian gatherings. I considered myself broadminded and tolerant without diluting or compromising my own faith.

At one point I made a list of some, not all, of the churches and Christian entities with which I had been involved in my lifetime: many kinds of Baptists, Methodist churches, Presbyterian, Pentecostal, Church of God, Mennonite, Christian &

Missionary Alliance, Moravian, Evangelical Reformed, Evangelical Free, Independent, Community, so-called Seeker Friendly Churches, Fundamental Bible, Covenant, Fellowship Bible, Bible Fellowship, Word of Faith, mega-independent churches, Healing Centers, Plymouth Brethren, Prophetic Word, Four Square Gospel, and Nazarene.

My husband and I were also involved in intercessory prayer movements and cell group churches. In China we worshipped in government-recognized churches and also with secret underground house churches. It was not because we were restless or dissatisfied; we weren't church hopping for variety or church shopping in a comparison study to find a perfect one. That would have been a mission impossible. We were honestly trying to cooperate with all of our brothers and sisters in Christ in the work of God's Kingdom.

Each of the above Protestant branches emphasized or perhaps over-emphasized some particular aspect of biblical truth but in so doing usually forfeited biblical balance. Most of these churches and groups did not claim to have some new revelation of foundational Truth. If they claimed new revelation, it would have been heresy. Their differences came primarily from individual interpretations of biblical doctrines by the leadership, some new applications of the once-revealed truth of God, or different ways of worship. They had no common ultimate authority to appeal to. Each branch has some of God's truth but not all of it. I respect the sincere intentions of the founders of each of these denominations and ecclesial entities and the work of the Holy Spirit through each of the Protestant branches. God is obviously using the many Protestant branches to either evangelize or build up some elements of society which might not be reached for Christ through other means.

In light of that, what was happening to me now? I was definitely not on a journey to seek new or different Truth. The truth I already knew was not insufficient, unsatisfying, or inauthentic. Rather, I was finding MORE of *the fullness* of the foundational Truth by which I had lived into my eighth decade. I was committed to "follow God *fully.*" This side of heaven I did not want to miss out on any of the wealth of Truth for which Jesus Christ gave His life and established His Church. If I wasn't open to understand and experience MORE, I would foolishly limit myself and try to limit God.

God's hand was on my life.

After experiencing multiple branches of the Christian faith throughout my lifetime, was it possible that my journey was at last leading me to the final fullness of Truth in the main trunk of the Christian tree? What was the main trunk?

I didn't start out to investigate the unfamiliar cobblestones in my life's roadway in order to make any changes in my own Christian beliefs or their practice! I set out to examine each unusual doctrine to prove that it was false or at best unnecessary to "make a highway straight for our God." So what was happening? The conclusions I was coming to were making my head spin.

Figuratively, my hand shook as I replaced the familiar rock, *sola scriptura*, on which I had stood so firmly and so long, with one labeled the *Deposit of Faith*. That *Deposit* still included inspired Scripture in its entirety but also incorporated authentic and historical Sacred Tradition. I could hardly believe how smoothly it fell into place in the gap in the roadway when I removed *sola scriptura*!

Chapter 4

ROCKING WITH
THE AFTERSHOCKS

Ladders and Leadership Levels

Just beyond the *Authority* boulder and lying in its shadow was a cluster of ecclesiastical stones.

Hierarchy and Church authority in general were unfamiliar concepts with which I began to grapple. In the past I had thought of hierarchy in negative terms. Perhaps I was reflecting the American or Western concept of the value of freedom from authority. After further study, I found that it was not a bad word, but indicated the orderly levels of leadership in any group relationship, church, or body of believers. In the Catholic context it refers to ordained leaders including the pope and bishops and their assistants, the priests and deacons, all of whom, the Catechism says, provide leadership through service.

Some sort of leadership ladder is familiar to most Protestants. However, it ranges from little or no accountability to multiple official rungs on the ladder of some of the more classic mainline denominations. Independent churches are known to spring up almost overnight, like mushrooms, with self-appointed leaders. They often make up their own statement of faith according to their personal interpretation of the Bible. That statement—if any—may echo the particular doctrinal emphases of the school in which the leader was educated. Converts or people who are attracted by the beliefs or practices of that local shepherd become his flock.

Although I'm reluctant to generalize, I've observed little hierarchy in evangelical churches. The trend seems toward independent congregations not connected to any larger faith network and answerable to no one higher on the accountability ladder. Each Christian, in fact, through personal Bible study and invoking the help of the Holy Spirit, is thought to be free to arrive at his own interpretation of Scripture. This echoes the legacy and liberty (and license) of the Reformation. Such churches may be governed by the pastor alone, by the congregation, by a group of elders, or by a board elected by members. Authority is usually vested in the immediate founders, the religious entrepreneurs who formulate the doctrinal statements and mission statements. Because most evangelical churches are not creedal, disciplinary action to maintain purity of biblical doctrine or moral behavior is difficult or rarely practiced. When attempted, it often leads to a church split. The person targeted for the discipline leaves and takes a part of the congregation along with him or her to start another church.

The Rock and the rock

Surprisingly, after I understood the biblical rationale for the *Deposit of Faith* and *Sacred Tradition* and discovered historically how it was passed on in the Early Church, other Catholic dogmas seemed less formidable. Since I familiarized myself somewhat with the writings of the Early Church Fathers, I understood from the careful exegesis of Matthew 16 that it must have been the man, Peter, whom Jesus called the Rock. It could not have been Peter's declaration of faith, as I was taught. Though other apostles were present, Jesus, the Good Shepherd, singled Peter out and gave him the mandate, "Feed My sheep"—but not until after Peter affirmed his love for Christ three times. Scripture records that Jesus gave to him as an individual the keys of His Kingdom and authority to lead the Church that Jesus would build. Jesus' promise that the Holy Spirit would guard the once-for-all Deposit of Faith and lead the future Church into all truth would activate that mandate.

It follows reasonably that Jesus expected to establish apostolic succession through the appointment of bishops and elders (priests) to carry forward the one, holy, apostolic Church through the ages until He would come again. I never thought I'd arrive at such a conclusion! However, I understood how logical and wise for the highest leadership of the worldwide Church to be vested in one man, the Bishop of Rome, the Pope, who would pilot the Church in concert with the Magisterium.

That latter term was certainly foreign to my Protestant thinking. I searched for the definition of Magisterium in the Catechism and found that it referred to the living teaching office of the Church. "Its task is to give an authentic interpretation of the Word of God, whether in its written form or in the form of Tradition. The task is entrusted to the bishops in communion with the successor of Peter, the Bishop of Rome [the Pope]. The Magisterium is not superior to the Word of God, but is its servant. It teaches only what has been handed on to it. At the divine command and with the help of the Holy Spirit, it listens to [the Word] devotedly, guards it with dedication, and expounds it faithfully." I read extensively on this crucial subject because it was so alien to my thinking.

Infallibility? That was a strange and rather large stone in the cluster, but it appeared reasonable when defined in light of the hierarchy as the gift given to the Church by Christ whereby it is protected from error on *essential matters of faith and morals*. It is most exclusively exercised by a pope or by an ecumenical council of bishops teaching in union with him. Infallibility is strictly limited to the above matters; it does not extend to pronouncements of the Pope or Catholic theologians or members of the hierarchy on any other matters. Jesus promised and guaranteed this protection through His gift of the Holy Spirit.

I originally thought that the word "catholic" was simply another denominational label. Actually, the meaning of the root word with a lower case "c" means universal or worldwide. I was coming to the point where I would have to decide whether or not I would acknowledge the Catholic Church to be distinct from all other churches and denominations: the "one holy catholic and apostolic Church" which Jesus established and promised He would build.

Sacraments was another big boulder to wrestle with on my roadway. As an evangelical I was familiar with certain purely symbolic rites—baptism and the Lord's Supper. We didn't call them sacraments; they didn't carry the sacred implications that the seven sacraments of the Catholic Church do. I learned that the seven sacraments are Baptism, Confirmation, Eucharist, Penance, Anointing of the Sick, Matrimony, and Holy Orders. A sacrament is defined as a special kind of sign that actually causes what it points to, what it represents.

By Water and the Spirit

Baptismal regeneration was a major stone lying out of place on my roadway. Baptism "is necessary for salvation; it forgives both original and personal sin and remits all punishment due to sin," as the Catechism states. Baptism "incorporates one into Christ's Body, the Church, and makes us children of God, and gives us the Holy Spirit and His gifts." Whoa! I had always believed that when you acknowledge that you are a sinner and accept Jesus Christ as your personal Savior, and if you truly mean it, you are born again on the spot, saved forever, and bound for eternal life in heaven.

Baptism, as I had always understood it, was a symbolic public act by someone who had already "accepted Christ." Since it was a "believer's baptism," infant baptism was ruled out except in certain classic denominations. Evangelicals differ in their belief concerning the necessity of baptism. For myself, I could now see from the biblical context that baptism is an essential component to salvation.

The Source and Summit?

How can Catholics believe that in the Eucharist or Communion during Mass the wine and bread, after being consecrated by the priest, actually become the flesh and blood of Jesus? However, from what I read, the sacrament of the Eucharist is the hub of Catholic faith. Once more I read John 6, which seems to be so important to Catholics. Jesus taught the necessity of "eating My flesh and drinking My blood" in order to "have life in you" and "have life eternal." That obviously caused many of His disciples to leave Him. Jesus did not call them back to explain that He was just talking figuratively. He allowed the literal meaning to stand. Nor in the institution of the Lord's Supper by Jesus in Luke 22:14-20 did He imply that He was using metaphors. As a matter of fact, neither did Paul in his account of that celebration among the first believers. Throughout the writings and oral teaching of the Early Church there is no question that they took the Real Presence of Christ in the Eucharist literally too.

I experienced another shock wave after the initial earthquake of replacing *sola scriptura* with the *Deposit of Faith*. If the Catholic Church was right about that and about baptismal regeneration, it could certainly be right again about the Eucharist.

Confession of sins to a priest along with absolution and penance? Another strange stone which I was at first inclined to toss aside. But when I carefully studied the biblical passages in John 20 and Matthew 16 where Christ clearly delegated authority to forgive sins to mortal men, the apostles, and by inference to their successors, I didn't know how else to interpret them.

Of course Christians may and should confess their sins directly to God according to 1 John 1:9, but there is apparently something more that Jesus had in mind when He established His Church. What does the Catholic Church mean by what it calls the Sacrament of Reconciliation? I was under the impression that it was the priest who forgave sins, but the Catholic Church doesn't teach that. After an individual's sincere repentance and oral confession, the priest pronounces God's forgiveness on the basis of Christ's merits alone and in Jesus' stead. The Church teaches that the priest's voice is heard, but when he says, "I absolve you," the "I" is Christ, not the priest.

Another aftershock! Familiar structures were starting to crumble all around me when I opened myself to an honest search for the Truth.

Another Disappearing Stone

When I started on my journey, I was certain that one of the large foundation stones on the familiar section of my road was nonnegotiable and permanent. But after I found more accurate information, *sola fide*, salvation by faith alone, faded away to a non-issue.

Many evangelicals believe that the Catholic Church teaches "works-righteousness," that one's salvation can be earned. Although denominational interpretations differ, evangelicals generally believe that we are saved by our *faith alone*. That is what I believed. That if one believes intellectually and also with the heart certain basic biblical truths and articulates them, that constitutes saving faith. It followed that one was justified before God, saved from eternal damnation, and guaranteed a place in heaven by that one act. I was sure that Scripture taught salvation by faith alone. But I discovered that there is only one place in the Bible where the phrase "by faith alone" appears, and it is a negative reference. James 2:24 declares, "See how a person is justified by works and *not by faith alone*."

I discovered further that the Catholic Church officially teaches that only by God's grace from beginning to end, completely unmerited by works, is one saved. God's grace justifies, sanctifies, and saves us. Further, the kind of faith that is mere belief in a list of propositions is insufficient for justification. Authentic, saving faith is always manifested in good works, but the initial justification still comes from faith, not from works. Good works by themselves aren't enough and neither is a bare faith in a list of propositions. If we have true faith, good works follow naturally and protect that faith.

I must admit that when all the facts were in, and the biblical references carefully exegeted in context, both of my lifelong foundation stones, *sola scriptura* and *sola fide*, disappeared. The reverberations from that shock wave made me dizzy.

The Saints Go Marching In

Meanwhile, I figuratively picked up a handful of the uncommon stones left on my roadway. There were still so many; even a few boulders remained. How could I possibly expect to examine, analyze, and make judgments about *all* of these unfamiliar theological stones? I was becoming really stressed because I couldn't discredit the Catholicism I had set out to debunk.

I still had the saints to explore—one of the biggest boulders. I expected to dispense with that subject quickly, however. It was a doctrine in which I had no interest and which I felt sure was "far out" without any biblical basis. Quite a number of questionables were clustered around the subject of saints. Looming so large in that cluster that it almost overshadowed my cobblestone road was the formidable boulder of Mary. Oh, Mary! She seemed as large as the Rock of Gibraltar. I remember reading someone's reply to the question of what were the greatest hindrances to her acceptance of the Catholic faith. She answered, "There were three: *Mary, Mary,* and *Mary.*" I could echo that. "Mary, Mary, quite contrary" as the children's rhyme goes. Certainly I had nothing against her personally. I didn't really know her, nor did I feel the need to get acquainted. Yes, she was Jesus' Mother, but I simply didn't see what all the Catholic fuss and focus was about.

First, I would establish what the Bible teaches about saints. All living Christians seem to be called saints by the writers of the New Testament epistles. The word means "holy ones." Not because Christians are already perfect while on earth, but they are pressing on to become like Christ. God calls us all to be holy. In the Catholic Catechism the word "saints" also refers to Christians who have departed this life. "Some of these saints may be our own deceased friends and relatives," declares the Catechism. Catholics believe that Christians who have departed this life are still very much alive in Christ because Jesus said that "they shall never die." Evangelicals would agree. But in an expanded way, the Catholic Church teaches that membership in the invisible Church is not terminated at death. The doctrine of the *Communion of Saints* implies that all God's people form one body in Christ (Romans 12:5) and share one another's gifts. Catholics believe that communion among us all, living and departed, continues without end.

The Catholic Church uses the term saints for special holy people, men and women through the ages whom the Catholic Church has canonized, that is, officially recognized for heroic virtue. I found that where the real difference between Catholics and evangelicals surfaces is whether the prayers of saints in heaven should or can be requested by the living, and whether we can or should pray to them. I thought I had finally found something contrary to Scripture! Doesn't God forbid prayers to the dead? However, according to Catholic doctrine, this communication with the departed is never for the purpose of foretelling the future or seeking information, which is certainly forbidden in Scripture. Foiled again!

Scripture does not tell us specifically or entirely what the "living saints" in heaven are doing throughout eternity. We learn from the book of Revelation that they are worshiping, adoring, and praising God, but it would not be inconceivable that they may also be praying for us as they did while on earth. I had never considered this. The view of evangelicals toward the departed is that we accept closure. We do grieve for our loved ones, of course, and we miss them and remember them; but we think of them as now beyond our reach. We believe that it is inappropriate and unnecessary to pray for them because their lives are over and nothing can be changed.

All it really says in Hebrews 9:27, however, is that "it is appointed that men die once, and after death be judged." When is that judgment? At the moment of death? At some point on our way to heaven? After we arrive in heaven? However, nothing unholy can even *enter* heaven (Rev. 21:27).

Evangelicals imagine that departed Christians are so taken up with praising God and enjoying the glories of heaven that they have neither the desire nor the ability to be concerned about people or affairs they left behind or anything else that happens on earth. I have to admit that is pure speculation. In contrast, the Catechism states, "We believe that those Christian heroes in heaven whom we call saints are vitally interested in those of us who are still living or in purgatory being purified [before moving on to heaven]. The saints pray for us in our weakness. And for our good, they offer the merits they earned on earth through Jesus, our one Mediator and Savior.... We also believe in the value of prayer for our departed brothers and sisters who are in purgatory."

I came to understand that Catholics venerate, that is, honor these men and women. They do not pray to the saints as though they were God. Rather, they petition them to intercede on their behalf with their heavenly Father since they are living in a deep, personal, and loving relationship with God. They pray to the saints to befriend them, too, especially those to whom they feel particularly close. They ask these personal heroes to take their petitions to the Father. They are also inspired by the example of their lives.

The Catholic Church doesn't teach that saints can directly intervene in our lives or actually answer our prayers. They simply pray for us to God. Just as we can't generalize about what all evangelicals believe and practice, it seems that some Catholics take certain pious practices beyond what Church dogmas spell out. That applies to devotional practices concerning both Mary and the saints.

This view of saints was strange to me as an evangelical but difficult to refute from Scripture or to prove from silence. From my study of the Early Church Fathers who succeeded the apostles, it was clear that communion with and prayer for "the living dead" was commonly practiced. During my teens I recited the Apostles' Creed in the Presbyterian Church. "...I believe in the communion of saints...." No one explained what that meant. I thought it might refer to the Lord's Supper, the Communion, or to the fellowship we enjoyed when Christians got together. Nor did anyone explain what we Presbyterians meant when we recited in the Creed, "I believe in the holy, catholic church...." I've been reciting and believing that Creed for a long lifetime!

Cloud of Witnesses

From the time I started on this journey I sensed that I was not alone. On both sides of the cobblestone road there seemed to be "a great cloud of witnesses" surrounding me and cheering me on (Hebrews 12:1). Who are they? I can't see them with my eyes, but they appear to be very much alive. It is as though they encourage me to keep going, assure me that God is leading me and will not forsake me or lead me astray. Actually, they seem to be praying for me! I feel hopeful and supported although I still don't know my destination.

Could these witnesses be some of "the living saints" in heaven? Possibly Christians whom I knew when they were on earth?

Or family members from my genealogical lineage? Or some Christians in the religious history of centuries past whom I researched for my autobiography?

I thought of my paternal grandmother, Frantiska, the primary Christian influence of my childhood. She was a saint if there ever was one. She died more than sixty years ago; I had always thought of her as dead now and beyond any communication. I recalled several strange incidents during my weeks of travel and speaking several years ago while promoting my newly published autobiography. In three different meetings in separate geographical locations where I spoke, strangers approached me with similar comments. "Your grandmother knows what you have written; she is pleased with you." At the time I didn't pay attention to those remarks.

Could Grandfather Jan and the other Christians in my generational past be part of this "cloud of witnesses"? Are they among the saints who are praying for me at this critical juncture of my life?

Then I had a sudden flash of memory—I was told by relatives that my Catholic grandfather, Jan, was a *stonemason* by trade. He worked on cutting stones, shaping them, and making roadways. Was he helping me along on my spiritual cobblestone roadway by his prayers from heaven?

Last of All—Mary!

I couldn't avoid her any longer. I had to deal with Mary. Formidable boulders remained, and many uncommon stones were still scattered on my pathway. None was as daunting as Mary, the mother of Jesus. We evangelicals were inclined to give her a respectful nod at Christmas and move on. At most we think of her as the privileged human channel for the incarnation of Jesus. Her prophetic declaration "All ages to come shall call me blessed" (Luke 1:48) goes over our heads and does not factor into our theology or devotional practice.

If we think about Mary at all, we shake our heads at the seemingly out-of-proportion manner in which Catholics worship her. Don't they have statues of and shrines to Mary, burn candles to her, endlessly pray the Rosary to her, and in so many ways permit her to detract from the primary worship due to Jesus? It seemed to me that Mariology diminished the exalted position of Jesus. Perhaps evangelicals are somewhat deficient in their view of Mary, but to regard her as "Mother of us all"? No way. Evangelicals accept the prophesied virgin birth of Christ as essential to the Incarnation—period. We acknowledge that Mary filled her role well and completed her mission.

Around Mary there seemed to be another cluster of intimidating stones: Immaculate Conception, perpetual virginity, her Assumption, her titles of Queen of Heaven and Earth, Queen of Angels, Mediatrix, Benefactress, Our Lady, Mother of God, Mother of the Church, the New Eve, The Immaculate, and the new Ark of the Covenant. Many Catholics accord Mary a special place in salvation history as Co-Redemptrix, although this is not a dogma of the Church. This all seems so unbiblical to evangelicals, even blasphemous.

I observed that many of these beliefs stemmed from the Catholic interpretation of the woman crowned with twelve stars in Revelation, Chapter 12, which they believe to be Mary. Evangelicals interpret it differently. From some of the programs I viewed on the Catholic TV channel, it seemed to me that the faithful look upon Mary as somehow more understanding, more generous and more approachable than her Son—more "user-friendly" for intercession.

As I sought to be fair and at least understand the doctrines of Mary in the Catholic Church, I delved into the Catechism and read widely in other books and in early church history. I found that Mary was actually not worshiped as though she were divine. She was and remains a fellow mortal. True devotion to Mary honors her; Catholics worship God alone. When they honor Mary, they are really thanking and praising God for blessing one of their mortal sisters. Mary's role as our mother is not meant to hide Jesus' role as our One Mediator. She uniquely points us to her son. Jesus gave his mother to all people everywhere to serve as their spiritual mother (John 19:27).

Catholics ask Mary to take their requests to Jesus as she did the problem of the lack of wine at the wedding in Cana (John 2:1-12). They believe that Mary is with God and has access to her Son; she can hear us, and she cares. They explain that she is the Mother of God only in the sense that Jesus is God (both God and man) and she is His mother. As a created human, Mary is not the mother of God the Father, of course.

Mary has not been part of my devotional life. To have anything to do with her is still a foreign concept to me as I explore the truth. However, after extensive reading with an open mind, I am beginning to understand where Catholics are coming from regarding some of those unfamiliar clustered stones of beliefs around Mary. To try to understand is already a significant step of logic and reason for me. My response of honest integrity keeps me open to welcome a closer relationship with Mary as time goes on.

The Eschatology Boulder

Having come this far on my journey, I was able to continue walking over some of the unfamiliar stones on my roadway without too much stumbling. Some of the previous problem stones were settling nicely into the gaps in my belief system. When I came around the next bend in the road, I drew back as I encountered a boulder I had never anticipated. The eschatology boulder looked vastly different from the smooth, well-polished prophetic roadway to which I was accustomed as an evangelical!

For a lifetime I had accepted without personal critical study the neatly diagramed and charted biblical end-times scenarios that prophetic Bible teachers offered so confidently. Of course those teachers still disputed among themselves and set up different prophetic camps flying different flags. I attended my share of rah-rah prophecy conferences through the years. Before me now stood a stripped-down, simple, Catholic, end-times boulder. Anyone embracing that would have a radically different view of the present era of unfolding history and of the ages to come than was depicted on the evangelical prophecy charts.

I searched for some kind of definitive, Catholic, end-times prophecy chart. I couldn't find one. The Catechism didn't even have a section on prophecy. Don't they have it all spelled out clearly like the evangelicals? We have the same Bible, after all.

I found one similar doctrine. The Second Coming of Christ is affirmed with every declaration of the Apostles' Creed, the Nicene Creed, and at Mass with the response: "Christ has died; Christ has risen; *Christ will come again.*" We share this important, nonnegotiable truth (1 Corinthians 15:23; 1 Thessalonians 4:15-17; Matthew 24:3-14; 2 Peter 1:16). We

61

also share the anticipation of Christ's imminent return.

The Catholic Church teaches that human history will come to a close when Jesus comes again at the *Parousia*, a word that means "presence" or "arrival." When this takes place, everyone who ever lived will recognize Jesus as Lord of all. The Catholic Church, however, teaches that Jesus will come visibly in all His glory, not secretly. The entire world will see Him, and God's reign will be fully established on earth. There is apparently no room in Catholic teaching for what some evangelicals call "The Rapture." According to that teaching the Church will not be snatched away into heaven by Christ to escape the great trials that are to come upon the earth. In essence, evangelicals are expecting a "third coming," although they would probably deny saying it that way.

From that point, Catholic end-times teaching swerves still further from the evangelical perspective. The Catholic Church interprets Revelation 20:1-5 as referring to Christ's spiritual reign in the Church and takes the term "a thousand years" to mean an indefinitely long time, not a literal one-thousand-year period called "the millennium."

My mind was reeling with the possibility that the pat and pet end-times scenarios which I had taken for granted might have other interpretations and still be biblically sound. I set about to pursue some serious study about the history of the Rapture teaching. It was really unsettling to find that it was not until the mid-nineteenth century that the premillennial view (Christ will come in a secret Rapture to snatch away true Christians to heaven before the Tribulation) and dispensational theology were first clearly formulated. Moreover, such teaching is almost exclusively an American evangelical interpretation. It was unknown in the Early Church, not taught through the ages, and unheard of even by the Reformers—yet I believed it for a lifetime without questioning its validity.

Something so mind-boggling and different from my present eschatological view will require a lot more careful study and prayer. Wow! I can't take many more of such hazardous boulders!

Chapter 5

Up Close and Personal

At the next critical crossroad I encountered the glaring change of signpost once again. It startled me! This time the sign blinked with colored neon lights—an uncomfortable personal challenge:

"What Will YOU Do with the Truth?"

The signpost pointed at me. Arlene's decision to become Catholic was between her and God. He used her situation to catapult me to examine my own journey toward Truth. I was now forced to put my friend's destiny on the shelf and deal with Truth myself. What I had been exploring was of eternal significance to my own faith.

I still had a backpack full of questions.

If I found some different or enhanced truths about the foundations of my faith, if that demanded a paradigm shift in my Christian beliefs, would I drop my pursuit of the Truth midcourse? Would I dare ignore at the peril of my soul what I had discovered—or would I have the courage to continue my quest to its conclusion?

I looked in vain for a signpost that would read U-TURN AHEAD. Was there no way to escape without making a personal decision about the truths I was discovering?

Does My Road Have an End?

I asked myself how much more I would still have to read, study, and examine before I was convinced that there are some vital Christian truths I have overlooked. Am I going to keep up this scrutinizing of Catholic doctrines forever? Or have I reached a point of no return? How much more light does God have to show me? John Henry Newman warned, "Don't sin against the light." The Scriptures declare that he who knows to do good and does not do it commits sin. Early in my walk with God I heard the same admonition: "Light obeyed increases light; light rejected brings the night."

The drastic consequences of rejecting truth scared me!

Facing All My Questions

Looking back at the bumpy road I have traveled, I ask myself what it is that I am trying to do by engaging in this personal microscopic examination of all those unfamiliar cobblestones that lined my faith journey.

If I rely solely on myself to make the final judgment of what is true and what is not, am I guilty of continuing to decide matters of faith by private interpretation? I had always done so; that is the Protestant way. But we are warned against that arrogance in 2 Peter 1:20: "Know this first of all, that there is no prophecy of scripture that is a matter of personal interpretation." Am I leaning on my own understanding contrary to Proverbs 3:5-6? Am I not in the rut of the misguided freedom of the Reformation that was foreshadowed in the times of the Judges in the Old Testament when "every man did that which was right in his own sight"?

The Reformation not only separated itself from papal authority and the Magisterium, but it continued separating within itself. Private interpretation tends to run wild. Hasn't following that principle resulted in the proliferation of tens of thousands of "small popes" believing that authority was vested in themselves? How else to account for the burgeoning number of denominations and churches, each asserting that it has the correct interpretation of Scripture?

Is the Holy Spirit confused or impotent? Did He disobey Jesus' promise and abandon the Church? Without authentic apostolic authority, many independent megachurches are appointing for themselves bishops and prophets of self-established congregations. Some even adorn themselves with gaudy priest-like vestments and command a large following.

Lord, to Whom Shall I Go?

What authority remains for the evangelical church? If it is Scripture alone, apostolic church history does not validate that. Authority continues to rest ultimately with any individual who claims that the Holy Spirit guides him to interpret Scripture.

My detailed exploration boils down to what or whom do I accept as authority? Myself? How can I trust my own reasoning power?

If I acknowledge from Scripture that Jesus established valid authority for His Church before He departed from His apostles, how can I justify ignoring His appointed authority? If I trust the *Deposit of Faith* passed from Jesus through the apostles and subsequently to and through the appointed leaders of the Early Church and on through the centuries to the present, can't I accept that the Holy Spirit did give careful supernatural oversight to that Truth through the Church? Didn't Jesus proceed to build His Church? Scripture is clear that establishing One Church was His sovereign "Plan A" for the perpetuation of the true faith and the propagation of the gospel and His Kingdom until He returns.

Did His "Plan A" fail? Was the Holy Spirit powerless against heresies and error? Did the Spirit allow the faith once purely delivered to be corrupted during those early years? Did the Church miscarry pure Truth so miserably that fifteen long centuries would pass in darkness and delusion before it was "reformed"? How could the Protestant Reformation with its resulting scattered, disunited flocks be God's beautiful alternate "Plan B"?

A Holy Church of Clay Pots

Of course the divine institution of the Church as the Body of Christ is composed of human beings subject to frailties and errors in judgment and behavior. Jesus fills His Church with "earthen vessels" that carry His precious Living Water. No one denies that there were corrupt, weak, self-seeking and flawed men who led the Catholic Church at times; likewise there are flawed and less than holy evangelicals and Protestants in today's multitudes of churches. Regardless, Jesus assured His apostles that the Holy Spirit would "guide them into all truth." Therefore, either I believe that the Spirit preserved the *Deposit of Faith* from error as far as faith and morals are concerned, or my Christian faith is a travesty and a fantasy. In that case, it would not be worthy of my belief, and eternal life would be an illusion and a sad and most pitiful dream.

Here I Stand!

If I settle the big boulder of *Authority* once for all, the entire cluster of strange-to-me stones around it should fit into place. How simple can it be? If I accept the reliable and God-ordained Authority vested in the Catholic Church, in the Vicar of Christ, and in the Magisterium, should I not believe and trust whatever it teaches?

I might never fully understand every facet of the Church's dogmas. In fact, I cannot; moreover, I don't need to. But I can accept those teachings in their totality by faith and without reservation because of the authority behind them, which is nothing less than the delegated authority of Jesus Himself. Didn't He tell the apostles, "Whoever hears you, hears Me"? That isn't blind acceptance without reason on my part. I don't turn off my intellect. Rather, it is my willing assent of true faith and trust in God.

Scripture warns against being double-minded. Surely God doesn't intend that I should travel to Heaven over two divergent sections of roadway. Nor is trying to walk on the median acceptable. In Jesus Christ "Crooked ways are made straight and rough places made smooth." God's way is one integrated surface. Jesus said, "I am The Way, The Truth, and The Life" and He prayed, "...that they may be ONE."

It has become obvious to me that only on such a roadway can I walk confidently as a pilgrim to the eternal destination where God wants to lead me. I continue to walk with the same precious Jesus whom I have known and loved for a lifetime. I am in the company of fellow pilgrims in the visible Body of Christ, the Church. The invisible "cloud of witnesses" along my path is cheering me on to the Promised Land!

So what am I afraid of? What is holding me back from making that broad jump from my evangelical faith comfort zone across the line to the uncharted territory of the Catholic Church?

Do I doubt that *God's hand is on my life?*

Chapter 6

STILL HUGGING THE FAMILIAR BANK

The Tiber River is a real river in Rome. To speak of crossing it often symbolizes one's decision to become Catholic. During my pilgrimage to Rome a few months after being received into the Church, I took a photo of the bridge spanning it and walked across in real time; I didn't have to wade or swim across the river.

While on my faith journey, however, I spent an inordinate amount of time pacing the bank before I decided to cross the Tiber. This side of the bank was familiar; what I would encounter on the opposite bank was unknown and scary.

Lifelong Catholics may not appreciate how traumatic and terrifying it is to make the leap from lifelong evangelicalism to Catholicism. Several analogies came to mind: I stand at the end of a diving board, and I'm being urged to jump. But I am not sure there is water in the pool! The feeling in the pit of my stomach might be like that of a trapeze performer high up in the circus tent just before he lets go to leap toward his partner who swings toward him on another trapeze. Will he and his partner perfectly synchronize to grasp hands in midair? I question whether there will be warm and welcoming Catholics to grasp my hands if I come into the Church. I don't see any safety net under me; there is no margin for error. Once I leap, I can't leap backward.

Such a decision is also like abandoning my birth citizenship to pledge allegiance to a foreign country that I once considered an enemy. As a deeply committed Protestant, I was facing the dismantlement of my entire faith universe, so to speak. Evangelicalism is a vast worldwide network in which I had been heavily and happily involved for scores of years. Leaving it would be like an astronaut stepping out of the shuttle into space without a tether.

There were moments when I asked myself: What am I thinking? Isn't this the season of my life to relax in my tried and proven faith and not rock the boat? Why not peacefully sail to the final harbor in my familiar boat? Why become like a salmon trying to swim upstream?

With what am I still struggling? I already changed my attitude to one of greater understanding and tolerance toward the Catholic faith. Can't I let it go at that? I don't have to go so far as to publicly change my affiliation to another part of the same Body of Christ. Can't I have it both ways? Can't I hang in at my theological comfort zone as a lifetime evangelical while I pick and choose from newly discovered and expanded biblical and Sacred Tradition truths? Can't I synthesize my faith? Can't I "eat my cake and have it too"?

Surely no one could fault me for my reluctance to make such a quantum leap to become a Catholic after a lifetime as a Protestant! I could never visualize myself sitting in that chair opposite the host, Marcus Grodi, on the live *Journey Home* television program and declaring to literally millions of worldwide viewers that I am now a Catholic. (Never say never! I did that very thing two years into my Catholic life!) I felt cold sweat even to think about applying the "C" word to myself. In a similar way I had shuddered even to pronounce another "C" word—"cancer"—when I went through that traumatic physical ordeal some years ago.

The Protestant evangelical branch I was presently on was sturdy, connected to the Christian Tree, and bearing good fruit. The spiritual sap which flowed into it did come from the Catholic Trunk. I believed that staying with my present branch would bring me to Heaven because of my sincere faith in the crucified and risen Christ and His sacrifice for my sins. I experienced God's forgiveness, had a personal relationship with Jesus, was secure in my love for Him, desired to obey Him, and the Holy Spirit lived in my heart. By grace I was saved!

Did I really have to swing off that branch and embrace the main trunk? No one was coercing me to make such a change; it was a matter of my own conscience.

Why does the Catholic Church call those branch Christians of whom I am a part "separated brethren"? It claims love and tolerance and respect for those outside its fold but at the same time wants to bring the wandering sheep back home into the main fold, the Catholic Church.

I continue to have the utmost appreciation for the evangelical branches that nurtured and sustained me throughout my life. I would not disavow, discard, or repudiate the precious foundational truths of biblical faith and the gospel which I learned as an evangelical and which I taught to others.

True, I can no longer be a *protest-ant* in relation to the Catholic faith. That label no longer fits me. Couldn't I be some kind of back-door Catholic apologist and defend their doctrines while remaining an evangelical? Could I perhaps be a "Catholic evangelical"? Couldn't I love both families of God and try to foster understanding between them? Or perhaps call myself a "completed evangelical" as some "completed Jews" do when they accept Jesus as the Christ, the Messiah?

I felt dizzy with all this personal cross-examination. Haunting me in the back roads of my mind, however, was the suspicion that to make no decision is a decision.

It all came down to this: What does Jesus want me to do? I want to please Him above all things. He is the Head of the Universal Church, His Body. It is His prerogative to place me wherever He wills in His Body and also to change my place as He wills. At this late stage of my life I can't afford to make a mistake. Jesus declared that His sheep hear His voice and they follow Him, and a stranger they will not follow. Early in life I promised with all my heart, "Where He leads me, I will follow." As one of His sheep, I need to hear His voice loud and clear. If I could only hear it distinctly, if I could really hear Him call my name, none of the other voices would confuse or frighten me.

Other Troublesome Questions

In retrospect, several major hurdles loomed before me as I lingered for an inordinately long time on my familiar evangelical bank of the Tiber River gazing across into *Catholicland*. The first monumental obstacle was the seeming impossibility of making such a change in the late years of my life, at the eleventh hour, so to speak. I had a fear of change! That fear is called *metathesiophobia*. A close second was my precious treasure. Oh, not money or material possessions. My lifetime "treasures" were my solid reputation as an evangelical and my visible positions in church and ministries. I was still involved in a worldwide network of evangelical coworkers and friends and mission connections.

I was cofounder of a now extensive evangelical mission organization thriving for nearly half a century and cofounder and president of a Protestant Christian radio station. My husband and I also founded a Chinese church in the nation's capital, which also has been successful in reaching an international community for fifty years and now has reached out with branch churches. I was an evangelical speaker and writer. I was afraid that the many books I had published would lose their market if I became Catholic, and I might be blacklisted as a speaker.

I risked losing treasured Protestant friends and disrupting my close family relationships. I would face misunderstanding and criticism and probably disappoint those who looked up to me as an evangelical. Those are all "biggies" when you come to the chronological summit of your life.

I identified with the rich, young ruler and the rich, old ruler, both of whom came to Jesus seeking deeper eternal truths and experience.

Jesus demanded of the rich, young ruler, "You've done well. But now sell all! Come follow Me...." I am old in years now, but I was afraid Jesus was still asking me to do the same thing. Both issues that held me back seemed like insurmountable obstacles.

Jesus cautioned us to count the cost. Would I be willing, if necessary, to sell all that I had, all my "treasures," to obtain the field where the Pearl of Great Price was buried, as Jesus taught in one of His parables? If the treasure turned up in an unexpected place, would I still pursue the spiritual fullness that beckoned me?

Both of my obstacles were present in the rich, old ruler, Nicodemus, who came to Jesus secretly after dark, as recorded in John, Chapter 3. Age and status and reputation were doubtless in the forefront of his thoughts; consequently, he could not risk asking his questions in public by daylight. For the same reasons

I was conducting my search clandestinely. It must have seemed to Nicodemus that Jesus was describing a ridiculous scenario. So he asked whether a man when he is old could reverse the natural sequence of life and "return to his mother's womb and be born over again." How could Jesus expect a seasoned, mature person, especially one in religious leadership, who has earned all the benefits of age and experience and is hopefully full of wisdom, to discard it all and start over like a newborn baby?

No wonder that seemed foolish to him. Nicodemus was a Pharisee with a reputation he must have deserved since John made a point to record that he was a religious leader, a member of the supreme Jewish council, the Sanhedrin. In Mark 8:31 Jesus foretold that He "must suffer greatly and be rejected by the elders, the chief priests, and the scribes and be killed." (This was fulfilled in Mark 14:53.) Those three categories made up the seventy-one members of the Sanhedrin, which was presided over by the high priest. Nicodemus apparently held a high position in that prestigious religious body. He would be taking an even greater reputation risk were he to follow Jesus than would the rich, young ruler.

If God called me to be a Catholic this late in life, could I make such drastic changes? Could I risk being responsible for possibly redirecting the Christian destiny of my descendants beyond my lifetime? Would I disillusion and confuse my family, my co-workers in ministry, and my evangelical friends with such an unexpected late switch of my faith context even though it was certainly still within the Body of Christ?

At the very least, heads might shake sadly with suspicion and pity that senility had overtaken me, that I might not be accountable for my deteriorating thought processes! Some might think that I had been brainwashed by too much study in the wrong direction and opened myself up to error. People usually look upon brainwashing in a negative sense. The way I viewed it was that my brain was being washed, but it was to cleanse me from my prejudices, misunderstandings, and misinformation. I consented to and welcomed that.

I realized I was indulging in "what ifs" and crossing bridges before I came to them, but I perceived them as realities.

On the other hand, it was possible that my family, relatives, and friends might not even care about any faith adjustment with which I was wrestling. What I experienced as an earthquake in my faith orientation they might shrug off as a slight tremor of little consequence. Why take it so seriously? How could I expect them to understand all the twists and turns of my theological journey, and why it was such a spiritual trauma for me?

Evaluating the Nicodemus Factor

Dietrich von Hildebrand (1889-1977) was a German Catholic philosopher and theologian whom the late Pope John Paul II called "one of the great ethicists of the twentieth century." He explored the problem of one's ability to change in mature years in his book *Transformation in Christ*. Age is often associated with resistance to change, a desire to settle in one's comfort zone, retirement from active life, and coasting quietly to a finish. To the elderly, security and *status quo* usually assume great importance. They covet a circle of like-minded friends; rocking boats is not a hobby they are inclined to pursue. The elderly have ingrained lifetime beliefs and habits that appear to be chiseled in stone. They've earned their reputation and guard it tenaciously; they are too tired to row upstream. They don't want their world turned upside down.

Von Hildebrand notes that love of change and daring is

the natural gift of youth, but when men become older, their characters and peculiarities solidify. In older years we are less receptive to fresh stimuli, and it is more difficult to revise our mentality and re-educate ourselves. We become rigid and the *natural* readiness to change diminishes. We settle down in the familiar. Von Hildebrand says that an aging person feels that he has the right "to be no longer a pupil or an apprentice but a master."

In contrast, "*Supernatural* readiness to change should grow with age." That is a surprising, optimistic declaration!

Von Hildebrand says that the supernatural picture will be different, and an inverse law will appear; receptiveness toward Christ will tend not to vanish but to increase as we grow into the later seasons of life. Incidentals recede into the background and the most important aspects of life become clearer. The restlessness of youth lessens, and "a steady orientation toward the essential and decisive becomes dominant."

He maintains that those advancing in age move toward supernatural simplicity; the closer we come to the gates of eternity, the more we understand "the one thing necessary." Those mature in years have a greater yearning for the depths of intimacy with Christ thus implying eternal youth in a supernatural sense. He explains that this leads to a supernatural readiness to change, to become a new person, to a willingness to crucify the old self.

That insight gave me a new, positive spin on the possibility of spiritual change in mature years with which I was struggling. What is *naturally* improbable in mature years is *supernaturally* normal and an action of the Holy Spirit toward transforming one into the image of Christ. So my late-in-life major faith paradigm shift is neither strange nor impossible in Christ!

What to Hold or Let Go

When I was initially struggling with my reluctance to abandon my loyalty to the *status quo* and comfort zone of my Protestant evangelicalism and my allegiance to the community of believers with whom I had served in ministry for a lifetime, it would have been an encouragement to read von Hildebrand's insight that "Fidelity to error is not a virtue."

He explains that to abide by a thing inflexibly, merely because we have once believed in it and have come to love it, is not in itself praiseworthy. We only owe our allegiance to truth and to genuine values. On the contrary, in regard to all errors and negative values, we should break with what we formerly cherished and withdraw our loyalty from them, once we know them to be false and negative in worth.

He further expands on hindrances to change by pointing out the dangers of feeling that we are obliged to be faithful to false ideas and ideals even after we have found them to be wanting. We may be comfortable with old and familiar things merely because we have lived so long with them and because they are connected with memories of our childhood and home.

By no means do I want to imply that the truth of God as I knew and sincerely embraced it as an evangelical Christian was in error, false, or contained negative values and therefore was to be repudiated and forsaken. I simply believe it to be incomplete—that the apostolic Church guarded and passed on the fullness of truth.

So then, if the stakes are high enough, if a greater treasure than the one I have is available, neither my reputation nor the difficulty of change should hinder me. What an encouragement! Even dramatic change is possible for a Christian in the latter years of life because of the eternal supernatural youthfulness that von Hildebrand describes. I want to live in a continual state of unconditional readiness to change in the positive ways to which the Spirit of God has been leading me. I am still a born-again child of God on the journey Home with my hand in my Father's hand and trying to follow Jesus ever more closely. The journey is getting long, and my *chronos* time on Planet Earth is realistically growing short. I struggle between the urgency to hurry across the Tiber, if God is really beckoning to me, and my need to take my slow and careful time because of the high risk.

Three-Stage Progression

Every journey for Protestants into the Catholic Church is unique. Each comes to the Catholic door with a distinctive backpack. One person may initially kick at the door in anger and offense. Another may knock tentatively to find out what is really inside. Some make as if to pass by but are drawn through the door in spite of themselves.

Yet there is some similarity of progression for most converts that lies just under the surface even of their unconscious inquiry. Gilbert Keith Chesterton (1874-1936), a famous late-in-life convert to Catholicism, wrote brilliantly about what he viewed as three phases of conversion. This seems fairly typical of many converts. The exception would be those who are truly adversarial and resistant and would be happy to bring down the Church.

Chesterton writes: "The convert commonly passes through three stages or states of mind. *The first stage* is when he imagines himself to be entirely detached... [like] the young philosopher who feels that he ought to be fair to the Church of Rome. He wishes to do it justice; but chiefly because he sees that it suffers injustice... I [Chesterton] had no more idea of becoming a Catholic than of becoming a cannibal. I imagined that I was merely pointing out that justice should be done even to cannibals....

"*The second stage* is that in which the convert begins to be conscious not only of the falsehood but the truth ... It consists in discovering what a very large number of lively and interesting ideas there are in the Catholic philosophy... This process, which may be called discovering the Catholic Church, is perhaps the most pleasant and straightforward part of the business... It is like discovering a new continent full of strange flowers and fantastic animals, which is at once wild and hospitable... It is these numberless glimpses of great ideas that have been hidden from the convert by the prejudices of his provincial culture, that constitute the adventurous and varied second stage of the conversion. It is, broadly speaking, the stage in which the man is unconsciously trying to be converted....

"*The third stage* is perhaps... the most terrible. It is that in which the man is trying not to be converted... He is filled with a sort of fear...He discovers a strange and alarming fact... a truth that Newman and every other convert has probably found in one form or another. It is impossible to be just [fair or unbiased] to the Catholic Church. The moment men cease to pull against it they feel a tug towards it. The moment they cease to shout it down they begin to listen to it with pleasure. The moment they try to be fair to it they begin to be fond of it....

"All steps except the last step he has taken eagerly on his own account, out of interest in the truth... I for one was never less troubled by doubts than in the last phase, when I was troubled by fears. Before that final delay I had been detached and ready to regard all sorts of doctrines with an open mind... I had no doubts or difficulties just before. I had only fears; fears of something that had the finality and simplicity of suicide... It may be that I shall never again have such absolute assurance that the thing is true as I had when I made my last effort to deny it....

"At the last moment of all, the convert often feels as if...he is looking through a little crack or crooked hole that seems to grow smaller as he stares at it; but it is an opening that looks towards the Altar. Only, when he has entered the Church, he finds that the Church is much larger inside than it is outside....

"There is generally an interval of intense nervousness... To a certain extent it is a fear which attaches to all sharp and irrevocable decisions; it is suggested in all the old jokes about the shakiness of the bridegroom at the wedding... He wonders whether the whole business is an extraordinarily intelligent and ingenious confidence trick... There is in the last second of time or hair's breadth of space, before the iron leaps to the magnet, an abyss full of all the unfathomable forces of the universe...That anything described as so bad should turn out to be so good is itself a rather arresting process having a savor of something sensational and strange..." (*The Catholic Church and Conversion*).

The Church which Jesus clearly established as recorded in the Bible, being the destined and prepared home of all mankind, isn't simply a human construct for me to decide for or against by my human reason alone. It is not up to any puny man or woman to come to a conclusion about her claims—such as we might about a new scientific theory. Chesterton's observations totally resonated with me. He described my journey. The minute I stopped being unjust to the Church, she began drawing me with the supernatural powers of the Holy Spirit.

I looked in the rearview mirror. In my case, I had set out to dig for the truth about the Church in order to undermine the decision of a fellow Protestant friend turned Catholic. A shameful motive I admit, although underlying that I sincerely wanted to rescue my friend from what I perceived as theological error. In the process, I tried at first to be fair to the Church by investigating her claims firsthand. That was also a matter of pride in order to prove my own ability and integrity. Gradually, after diligent research and prayer, weighing every doctrine against Scripture, hoping to find it wanting, I did a turnabout. I started to defend her claims. I can't pinpoint exactly when I crossed over the median. After that, the supernatural magnet of the Holy Spirit began to draw me through the door in spite of myself.

Fears certainly gripped me as I neared the threshold. I spent the latter part of my four-year journey hugging the familiar near bank of the Tiber. It was not because I was a slow learner but because of the magnitude of the religious paradigm shift so late in my life. My decision had both temporal and eternal ramifications; I had to proceed with caution and thoroughness.

I never doubted, however, that *God had His hand upon my life*.

Chapter 7

ENCOUTERING A NEW FAMILY

Meeting Other Inquirers

To this point my journey had been a covert one. I hid in my two closets: the closet of prayer and the closet of secret research. I was too visible in the evangelical world to let anyone know I was researching Catholicism. Now I felt it was time to meet some flesh and blood Catholics and at the same time explore that faith with a group.

I called the local Catholic church in Winchester, Virginia and found that a class for inquirers was starting in September and would meet once a week. They called it RCIA, the Rite of Christian Initiation of Adults. The leaders assured me that I would not be obligated to become Catholic at its completion, but if I decided to, this class would prepare me.

In hindsight, I probably could have taken a short cut by meeting with a priest to receive individual instruction toward possible Confirmation. After all, I had read voluminously and studied for nearly four years on my own. Instead, I believed that God wanted me to slug it out for the whole nine yards—the full nine-month course. I would let my "pregnancy" go full term before birthing my Catholic faith.

The first evening that I stepped into the parish hall for classes, my heart was racing. I was actually in a Catholic church for the first time! Where would all this lead? I was the oldest student by far. Many in the class were beginners who barely knew the basics of the Christian faith that I had taught for a lifetime. It was a good review and good spiritual discipline. There I found solid biblical and historical and spiritual answers that helped me become oriented in a group situation. I was encouraged to find that I was not alone in my quest for truth or my questions.

I tried to keep secret from my family and close friends why I disappeared every Monday night week after week, but eventually it leaked out that I was attending Catholic instruction sessions. Friends became alarmed and tried to rescue me from error in the same way that I had pounced on my friend Arlene. I braced myself for further onslaughts that I was sure would come.

I continued to watch the *Journey Home* program on EWTN and videotaped every program to view again. It provided me with real-life examples of Protestant leaders who faced the same questions and had the courage to go public after they found the fullness of Truth in the Church. I kept reading widely in the Early Church Fathers, something I never did during my academic years.

Going to The Meal

One can load up with facts from written sources, but that is like studying a menu without ever going to the restaurant and enjoying the meal. I finally became bold enough to attend Mass incognito for the first time at Sacred Heart of Jesus Catholic Church where I was enrolled in RCIA. I had been forewarned not to expect Catholics to enthusiastically welcome a visitor, as evangelicals would have.

I slipped in and sat alone as far in the back of the sanctuary as I could; I tried to be invisible. The narthex (foyer) was always abuzz with happy fellowship after Mass among people many of whom probably grew up together. I guess I was invisible, since no one welcomed me during my initial weeks of attending Mass. Since I was prepared for that, it didn't bother me.

I chose the 11:15 Mass on Sunday, one of five weekend Masses offered in addition to two daily Masses. I sat transfixed through all the up and down activity and made no effort to participate. All the people around me seemed to know what they were doing and when to do it. I couldn't follow what was going on, and no one offered to help me through the maze. I felt like I did when I first arrived in China. I was in a foreign country without a guide or interpreter.

I didn't know what to expect. When we met for a "service" in an evangelical church, the main entrée was "the preaching of the Word." The more informal and seemingly unplanned a Protestant service is, the more people feel it is being led by the Spirit. Many churches no longer have a printed order of service or bulletin so you can expect almost anything. Written prayers, memorized prayers, creeds, recitations, or responses are virtually unknown except in some of the more traditional denominations. We expect the minister to deliver the sermon with few if any notes no matter how much preparation he puts into it. For him to read a sermon would be "evangelically incorrect." A sermon lasting at least a lively half hour or more is about average; in some churches, particularly Pentecostal, a whole hour of preaching is not unusual. The celebration of the Lord's Supper may take place during the service once a month, once a quarter, or once a year in some denominations.

I was accustomed to a praise team with orchestra or band instruments supplementing the choir which usually performs front and center. Songs expressing personal spiritual experience, often the newer short praise choruses sung multiple times, and contemporary music make for an atmosphere of unceremonious spontaneity in evangelical churches. Many congregations clap to songs and lift their hands in praise. Words of songs are projected on large wall screens; the use of hymnbooks is tapering off except in mainline Protestant churches. Congregations gather in rather simple, unadorned buildings that look more like auditoriums with stages where performances are held. Sometimes chairs are stacked up afterward and the meeting place turns back into a gymnasium during the week.

What a contrast at Mass! Liturgy overwhelmed me—I didn't even know what the word liturgy meant. I found out later when I checked the Catechism. It refers to "the interactive ceremony, all the activity and actions of people and priests that goes on at the Mass." Liturgy includes words, symbols, making the sign of the cross, genuflecting, prayers, singing by congregation and choir, blessings, reciting the creed, and confession of sin. Responses, kneeling, gestures of priest and people, reading of the Scriptures, adoration, meditation in silence are all part of the liturgy. So is praising God, celebrating, partaking the Eucharist, greeting with peace those around you, using holy water, burning candles, processions, offerings, thanksgivings, the ringing of bells, standing, sitting, bowing, incense, participation of laity, and altar servers—everything that has to do with the five senses. Yes, most of it was there when I attended my first ever Mass.

And wonder of wonders—only a five-minute homily (not what I would call preaching) by the priest whom they called "the celebrant"! It was a short commentary on or application of the gospel reading for the day. I was amazed to learn that the same Scripture selections are read at Masses worldwide in each country's native language. The Liturgy is said to call people to experience the mystery of salvation united with the saints in heaven and the angels who are worshiping God with many of the same words recorded in the book of Revelation.

"Canned or freeze-dried prayers," as Protestants sometimes refer to ready-made prayers, are seldom used by evangelicals who may assume God only listens to homemade spontaneous prayers. Even the Lord's Prayer is seldom recited in evangelical churches. In the Catholic Church, liturgy provides worshipers with the words to say and thus assists them to enter rightly into the corporate worship of the Church—or so I read in my resource books.

I felt a spirit of hushed reverence and quiet, devotional worship which I missed in many evangelical churches. I didn't hear the disturbing undercurrent of chatter in the congregation that I was accustomed to. Many people came early and spent time kneeling in personal prayer on the padded kneelers. (Crying babies and noisy toddlers somewhat disturbed the peace since entire families with many children in tow filled the pews. The family togetherness was, however, refreshing.) The sanctuary was conducive to worship with its beauty of architecture. From spectacular stained-glass windows to ritual gold altar vessels and colorful vestments of priests, the ministry of altar servers, chants, candles, statues, and the Crucifix—all invited adoration of God. I seemed to have stepped into a different world.

Protestants are inclined to view such appeals to the senses as distractions from the simplicity of the gospel and not really worshiping God "in spirit and in truth." Did God state His preference for the loud noise of boisterous praise? Apparently God approves of visual aids and object lessons since the Bible is full of them, and Jesus used them liberally. God created beauty and called it good. We were made in His image and I can understand that since He endowed us with five senses, we can and should use them to worship Him. The Old Testament was full of ritual, pageantry, spiritually meaningful ceremony, elaborate vestments, and prescribed liturgy. Solomon's Temple must have been splendid beyond description, lavish, extraordinary to behold, one of the great wonders of the world. Today's evangelicals might have thought it extravagant, excessive, and ostentatious. But didn't God dictate all of its details and design? The same criticism might be leveled against the magnificence of Catholic cathedrals, basilicas and shrines, but the beauty is obviously focused on the glory of God.

After subsequent visits to Mass, I was better able to follow the ceremony since it was always the same. The haze began to clear. I started to grasp the beautiful, sacred drama of the gospel that was being so reverently portrayed. Some vestiges of the liturgy in Latin were still used, and I regretted that I didn't pay more attention in Latin class in high school, although I wasn't sure it was the same kind of Latin we were taught when we learned to translate "Publius wore his new toga to the forum." Some of the liturgy was ancient, and the worship implications awesome and biblical. I was surprised to hear more Scripture at every Mass than in an average Protestant church service. Readings by laymen and laywomen were always selections from the Old Testament, from the Psalms, and from the epistles before the priest read from the gospels.

Most of the congregation lined up to go forward to receive in their hands or on their tongues the Eucharistic wafer, after which they returned to their pews. Many elementary school age children received the wafer as well. The priest touched in blessing the heads of the babes in arms and the toddlers who followed their parents to the altar.

Singing was from the hymnbook in the pew racks, no snappy choruses or screen-projected words; the choir and organist were upstairs in a balcony behind the congregation and not clearly visible to the people. I learned later that one of the Masses earlier on Sunday morning was more contemporary with guitar accompaniment, and the Spanish Mass in the afternoon was quite a bit more boisterous with brass instruments and lively singing.

I wasn't so naïve as to think that everyone at Mass was worshiping sincerely and participating with deep personal reverence and pure motive. Nor would that be the case in the average evangelical church. That is not for me to judge. Yet the contrast in level of reverence continued to move me deeply. I needed time to sort all this out in my own mind.

And Still Further Afield

After the third year of my investigation, I took courage to attend the Coming Home Network International conference in Ohio whose theme that year was "The Early Church Fathers." I decided to drive the day's trip and take on a new adventure. The knowledgeable speakers, some of whose stories I had heard on EWTN's *Journey Home* program, fleshed out the findings from my own research. The hotel where our meetings were held was full of converts to the Catholic Church and those still on the journey. I met more people like myself—we were a multitude! What sweet fellowship we enjoyed! There I found enthusiastic acceptance and understanding and yes, the people were "warm and fuzzy" huggers! Although I initially knew no one, after that weekend no one was a stranger; I felt that I was truly on the way Home.

One of the speakers was Rod Bennett from Atlanta whose book on the early fathers, *Four Witnesses*, I had devoured. We became friends and I was honored that he offered to be my theological mentor for my journey into the Church. I also requested a woman mentor and Dr. Robin Maas from the Washington, D.C. area was assigned to me. I gave both a really hard time during the final year of my journey. They were so patient and thorough with me. Since both mentors lived at a distance, we carried on all of our encounters in cyberspace by e-mail. I had the best personalized guidance. Several inches of our correspondence printouts were stacked beside my laptop by the time I was ready to come into the Church.

Are We There Yet?

A child on a long auto trip keeps nagging his parents, "Are we there yet?" So I began to wonder if I might die before I took the final leap into the Church! The problem wasn't a choice between Truth or Consequences, as in the children's game. I knew that consequences would be inevitable if I followed the truth; that troubled me. The Holy Spirit therefore led me gently and progressively because I needed to be thoroughly convinced intellectually, biblically, and historically. Later the spiritual and emotional assurance would come flooding in to confirm God's leading.

All my life I had been in process and in formation—continually being converted in the sense of being transformed. I hungered and thirsted and sought for MORE of the deep things of God ever since my childhood. God drew me on gradually to "taste and see" MORE and MORE. Now I was confronted with the full truth. My heart was touched by the words of a beautiful

Catholic hymn: "You satisfy the hungry heart with gift of finest wheat." The finest wheat was ground into the finest flour and baked into the finest bread—that bread was the Eucharist, the Body of Jesus given for me, His real presence.

Could it be true? Was I really headed to *The Land of MORE?*

God had His hand on my life—so He led me onward!

Chapter 8

TREASURES LEFT
ON THE SAND

Sunday, January 23, 2005 was one of those "best of times and the worst of times." I had no idea it would be my day of decision—but *God had His hand on my life.*

Snow had fallen steadily. The temperature dropped into the low teens with minus zero wind-chill. The winding slope of gravel driveway leading to the main road from the little chalet in the woods where I lived alone was frozen over and slippery. I didn't think it was safe to drive to Mass that morning. I had begun to go regularly although I had not made public any decision to become Catholic.

The date commemorated what would have been the eighty-ninth birthday of my late husband, Ted, who had died thirteen years earlier. I watched Mass on television and lit a candle for him. I spent part of the day remembering, with thanksgiving to God, our forty-six years of marriage, ministry, and parenting together.

In late afternoon, experiencing cabin fever from my isolation, I decided to risk driving out to 5:30 Mass at Sacred Heart. Almost immediately I experienced an upset stomach and the onset of a headache, which I seldom get. The temperature outside dropped still lower, the wind blew strong gusts, and I had ample excuses for backing down on my decision. Nevertheless, I felt a strange quickening anticipation of destiny—for some reason I had to get to Mass.

I took a Tylenol, bundled up in my down-filled jacket, boots, scarf, and ski cap and set off.

The moon shone brightly in the already dark, clear sky casting shadows as if it were sunlight. The road crackled and slipped under my tires as they spun to get a grip.

The sanctuary was almost full despite the weather. The Gospel reading from Matthew 4 included the account of Jesus' call to two sets of brothers in the fishing business. When Jesus called them to become disciples, all four left their occupations "at once." Father Krempa's homily expanded on their immediate response while my mind stayed anchored on what the Holy Spirit was speaking to me between the lines of Scripture.

The congregational hymns followed the theme of the calling of Christ to us personally. The last two phrases of the refrain of the post-Eucharistic hymn were,

All my treasures are left on the sand there;
Close to Thee, Lord, I shall sail other seas.

Those words pierced my heart. My eyes blurred with tears as I pondered why—why—was I still putting off my critical decision about embracing the Catholic faith? I am not an indecisive person by nature. Nevertheless, I was facing what to me was a monumental decision. I simply couldn't hurry it. I had to be absolutely certain of the truth.

Faith and reason had to be in synch if I were to make such a paradigm shift in my Christian faith. If I crossed that bridge over the Tiber, I thought I would have to burn all my bridges behind me. This late in life I couldn't afford a mistake; I figured that the rest of my life on earth and my eternal destiny hung in the balance.

I tried to convince myself that I had to test that decision with time so it would be a calm, informed, mature, and permanent one. Was I simply making excuses to put off commitment?

Wasn't the real problem whether I would accept the whole of the Catholic faith, the total authority of the apostolic Church? Not whether my intellect could understand each of its dogmas. I would have to accept that the Catholic Church teaches absolute truth by the authority of the living God, and that the biblical record is clear that the Church was established as His visible Body on earth by Jesus Christ. I would have to believe that the Holy Spirit was faithful and did guard and guide the Church into all truth.

My evangelical friends felt that I would be taking a giant step backward, that I would check my mind at the church door and give up my freedom to interpret Scripture for myself. However, I had begun to see it as taking a giant step forward into the fullness of God's truth.

I was tired of dragging my feet. Dissecting Catholic teachings one by one was like examining each tree but missing the beauty of the forest. I was weary of taking a mental magnifying glass and obsessively examining every Catholic doctrine, comparing it to my Protestant belief system and the biblical context. First I tried on Catholic eyeglasses, then Protestant ones, then bifocals. I found that interpretations of essential doctrines did differ between Protestants and Catholics, but I also discovered that there was more to revealed truth than I had previously realized. I encountered problems, but I also found satisfactory answers.

I was not a disgruntled, unhappy, confused, dissatisfied evangelical. I appreciated my biblical Protestant background. Even in that context, however, I always understood there was more and sought the fullness of objective Christian truth.

At the slow rate I was going, just how long might this faith exploration and examination take before I could be sure that I am sure of the truth of this fullness I was encountering? Forever, I realized, if I continued to "lean on my own understanding."

I sensed that tonight was showdown time. *God's hand was heavy on my life.*

The four future disciples never hesitated; they left their nets, their boats, their livelihood, their relationships, and their reputations. No second thoughts; they didn't drag their feet as I was doing.

When I was young and my boat and nets were new and empty and untested, I didn't hesitate to answer Jesus' call to follow Him, to trust Him unconditionally with my future. No mental reservations, no more proof needed that He was the Christ, the Son of the Living God. I committed my life to Him. I was sure that He would not lead me astray and would be my Guide for a fruitful Kingdom life as long as I would live. Jesus promised that He would make me a fisher of men.

Now I am old; my boat is weather-beaten, my well-worn nets are torn and in need of mending from much hard use. God is so good; He was faithful to His promise. My nets were filled and heavy laden with fish for scores of years.

How should I respond to Jesus' fresh, new call to follow Him into still deeper waters for a still greater catch of fish? Was He beckoning to me again near the end of my life to "bear fruit, more fruit, and much fruit?" Does God really expect me to remain "full of sap and very green" (Psalm 92:14) in old age? Would He exchange the weakness of my chronological age and my growing limitations for His strength (Psalm 103:6 and 2 Corinthians 12:9)? Was He leading me to still greener pastures and fresher waters in my eighties?

Surely I don't need any more proof of His lifelong faithfulness, of His Divine identity, or of the assurance that what He promises He always fulfills. God's track record in my life is flawless. I know that His "goodness and mercy" will continue to "follow me all the days of my life" and that I will "dwell in the house of the Lord forever..." (Psalm 23).

My Treasures Weighed in the Balance

So then, once for all, what shall I do about the so-called treasures that I accumulated during my lifetime? Is my Christian reputation as an evangelical such an important treasure? Such a trifling thing should not even concern me. It is not as if I were changing my faith. I am anchored in the entire Word of God—the Word taught, the Word written, the Word become flesh with whom I continue my intimate relationship.

Is my treasure the circle of friends and family and coworkers who may not understand or approve my seeming defection from their traditional practice of faith? Earthly relationships are short-lived! Obedience to God's leading is a higher eternal priority.

Is my treasure my missionary service overseas for God's Kingdom? Not worth mentioning—as His servant I have only done what I should have to spread His Kingdom.

Are my treasures the books I have written and published? I intended them to bless and help others—the fruit they are bearing I gladly lay at Jesus' feet. I can understand Saint Thomas Aquinas' comment after he experienced a special vision of the Lord. He immediately stopped his prolific writing and exclaimed: "I cannot go on... All that I have written seems to me like so much straw compared to what I have seen and what has been revealed to me."

I declare with Saint Paul, "Whatever gains I had, these I have come to consider a loss because of Christ. More than that, I even consider everything as a loss because of the supreme good of knowing Christ Jesus my Lord. For his sake I have accepted the loss of all things and I consider them so much rubbish that I may gain Christ and be found in him..." (Philippians 3:7-8).

So much for my treasures.

Now or Never!

I sense that Jesus requires an immediate response from me tonight to His call, "Follow Me." No more interminable weighing of pros and cons, gains and losses, seeking to understand every iota of Infinite Truth with my finite human mind. I will not inquire only to reluctantly back away like the rich, young executive who turned down Jesus' call with great sorrow because of the abundance of his treasures. What genuine treasures he could have enjoyed and passed on to the world as a disciple or apostle of the Lord! He might have been another Paul or a Peter. We don't even know his name! He was young and full of potential. I could make the same mistake when I am old if I use age or my treasures as excuses for not following Jesus fully to new horizons.

So then—YES! I accept Your will, Lord. I will follow You fully and without conditions!

"All my treasures I will leave on the sand there;
Close to Thee, I shall sail other seas."

Mass was over. Bundled up again in coat, scarf, and mittens, I went out into the dark, cold night. My breath blew frosty mist. The moon was a brilliant, silver orb and the stars shone like diamonds on deep blue velvet.

I blinked back tears but not from sorrow or regret or

hesitation. They were tears of exultation and joy because I had made my decision! The Holy Spirit drew me; God spoke—My Shepherd called me by name! I responded with the same *Fiat* that had bubbled from my soul when I was a teenager and first heard Jesus' call: "Follow Me and I will make you...." At that time I surrendered my brand new nets and followed Him immediately. True to His promise, He has been working on making me for nearly 80 years. I am still in process, in formation, being conformed, transformed to the image of Christ.

From that point on, I shoved off from shore with Jesus to "sail other seas" in deeper waters. At the Lord's command I willingly let down my worn nets once again. In my heart of hearts I crossed the Tiber that night although my public profession was to come later!

Chapter 9

SPRINTING TOWARD EASTER VIGIL

In the months that followed, my fellow classmates in RCIA also made their decisions whether or not to proceed toward being received into the Church the evening before Easter Sunday. Some felt they were not ready and along with others decided not to pursue their journey for whatever reasons. That was certainly their prerogative.

As for me, I couldn't run fast enough now that I knew for sure where God was leading me on this tortuous road! My journey hadn't been a walk in the park; I was not on a mere vacation trip or excursion. It turned out to be a spiritual pilgrimage with a destination I didn't expect. The cobblestone road led me to the bank of the Tiber River where I lingered longer than would seem necessary. But God was patient with me and let me take my time because *His hand was upon my life.*

Taking Stock of My Progress

I had a different perspective when I returned to my RCIA classes after my January 23rd milestone decision. I had come a long way to reach a place of reasoned understanding and surrender of my pride. At that point God generously imparted the gift of faith to me. He showed me that faith comes first; understanding follows. Faith replaced my skepticism when I acknowledged that there are mysteries only God knows and some things that I may never understand. Biblical and historical evidence convinced me, however. If the Church were accurate in her origin, I would trust what the Church teaches because the Holy Spirit protected revealed truth according to Jesus' promise. Period!

I could hardly believe what was happening to me. I now accepted spiritually and heart-emotionally as well as intellectually the very teachings which I initially opposed so strongly and tried to debunk! After being stalled for so long with my intellectual investigation, I could hardly wait for Easter Vigil. I was so eager for the time to come when with all my heart and soul and mind I would declare publicly: *"I believe and profess all that the holy Catholic Church believes, teaches, and proclaims to be revealed by God."*

I knew it would take the rest of my earthly life to obey the implications and live out the personal applications of all those rich apostolic teachings. I wanted to press on as far as possible and for as long as I had life and breath toward God's call to holiness and spiritual fruitfulness through the work of His Holy Spirit in my life. I was not under any illusion that I would reach the goal of perfect holiness. Even the apostle Paul wrote, "It is not that I have already taken hold of it, or have already attained perfect maturity, but I continue my pursuit in hope that I may possess it, since I have indeed been taken possession of by Christ" (Philippians 3:12). I had no doubt that at the end of my life I would still be far from God's perfection. But He wonderfully provided a way to complete my purification, which I was yet to discover.

A bridge across the Tiber stretched before me. On the other side of the bridge was *The Land of MORE* that I would not only explore but also where I would joyfully settle and be fruitful. It was still a foreign country to me, but it would become my Home in much the same way as China became my home after my husband and I arrived there for ministry. I had much to learn. At my advanced age I would have to enroll in an accelerated course!

To reach the other side I had to publicly cross the bridge; that would take place at Easter. I needed a "crossing guard" like schools provide for children on a busy thoroughfare. My RCIA leaders, Ed Norris and Paul Kielmeyer, and my two mentors-at-a-distance, Dr. Robin Maas and Rod Bennett, were my crossing guards to conduct me over the Tiber. They hung in with me and provided patient course correction and wise counsel for my everlasting questions. They were always ready with a list of helpful web sites for my research, excellent books to recommend, and biblical passages to plumb in greater depth. Their prayers held me steady as I moved along the bumpy cobblestone road toward my public profession. They warmed my cold feet, mopped my sweating brow, and held my trembling hands as the occasion warranted. They were my cheerleaders as well as crossing guards.

In the bleachers I had several surprise supporters from the evangelical ranks who cheered me on. Some whom I least expected let me know that they were "on my side" and respected my decision. They assured me that they trusted my lifelong track record of following God's will, and although they weren't interested in following my example, wished me well. They encouraged me with their understanding, continuing friendship, and open, loving acceptance as I stepped closer to the bridge.

Cat Out of the Bag

About six weeks before Easter Vigil, our RCIA leaders asked each of us to notify them how many places in the sanctuary to reserve for our family and friends. That forced me to decide whether the time had come to let certain friends and family members know of my decision before my Confirmation—or to wait and notify them afterward. My mentors cautioned me to be prayerful about whom to inform and when. They suggested that an advance announcement might immediately open me to more questions than I might have time or experience to adequately deal with at that point. In some cases, it might invite unnecessary opposition that could distract me at this critical time. On the other hand, it was not wise to treat my decision as if it were a secret.

I concluded that my immediate family, some extended family, certain relatives, close friends, and co-workers in ministry deserved a heads-up about this momentous and happy step in my faith life.

On my computer I designed a semi-formal invitation to attend my Confirmation Mass and the reception that was to follow. It provided the five "Ws" and would certainly let the cat out of the bag—for better or for worse. I knew that those who lived at a distance wouldn't be able to attend anyway; for them it would serve as a courteous announcement. Many others, probably after reeling from the initial shock, would not even want to attend, so seating in the sanctuary would not be an issue. I sent the invitation out to a selected list with a brief, personal cover letter alluding to my lengthy, thoughtful, and prayerful journey of exploring the Catholic faith. I assured them that I have not "jumped ship" from our Christian faith. Because of the need for a head count for seating on that customarily crowded prime event of the year and the reception, I requested an R.S.V.P.

My invitation opened a floodgate! I was suddenly besieged with phone calls, letters, e-mails, and personal visits mostly expressing strong opposition and criticism to my crossing that dangerous bridge. Some expressed shock, others bewilderment, still others sadness, disappointment, even tears. A few were actually angry and offered dire warnings of the consequences of what I was contemplating. Well-meaning evangelical friends literally tried to "head me off at the pass" to prevent my taking such a heretical step. Some wanted to engage in theological wrestling matches.

I could understand and sympathize with them because when I started off on my reluctant journey, I felt the same way toward my friend Arlene. What goes around comes around!

It reminded me of a certain mature-in-years Christian friend who tried to dissuade me from marrying my husband on the very night before our wedding! I was more than a little nervous when the minister came to the point in the ceremony, "If anyone here knows any reason why this couple should not be wed, let him come forward...." Thank God no one did! In the case of my being received into the Catholic Church, some who had not even received an invitation took it upon themselves to challenge me.

After I settled into my Home in *The Land of MORE*, and to the present time, controversy and misunderstanding about my embracing the Catholic faith have continued to dog my footsteps. Little by little, God taught me how to transform adversity into a continuing opportunity to offer a reasoned and loving witness and defense of God's full truth. At this early point in my journey, I confess to being inclined toward self-pity and applying balm to my bruises. As an evangelical, I was accustomed to being lauded and applauded and respected, certainly not criticized for anything that had to do with my Christian faith and life.

My Encrypted Calling Unfolding

Since I took my private step of faith that blustery, snowy day in January, I began to wonder about the larger picture of why God might be calling me at this late season of my life to change boats in the middle of the stream. I didn't think it was simply for my own spiritual benefit. Could God have some deeper reasons for my "Eleventh Hour" summons?

I shored up my courage and went more often to Mass. Since I was still on my journey into the Church, of course I could not receive the Eucharist. Nevertheless, I could participate in the rest of the Liturgy and sit under the teaching homilies of the priests at Sacred Heart. I grew brave enough to ask for an appointment with the senior parish priest, Father Krempa. In one homily he suggested that when God calls us to follow Him, He may have a hidden agenda for us, *encrypted* almost like code.

"God gives spiritual experiences not only for our own benefit but also to help other people and for reasons that may not be obvious," Father explained; God's purposes for our lives are mysterious, known only to Him. According to the definition of *encrypted*, the reason for secrecy is so that something will be "unintelligible to unauthorized parties" similar to a code to protect classified information. God deals with us individually and intimately, but as we walk in obedience to Him one step at a time, He will reveal His secret ways to us.

What is *encrypted* in God's call to me as I become Catholic? I strain forward in faith and eager anticipation to find out.

Father counseled me to pray and remain open to the specific spirituality and service which God will develop in me, one that will be most pleasing to Him for the building of His Kingdom. He suggested that it is likely to depend on my present state in life, my past experience, gifts, and the opportunities He would set before me. Since I am a writer, Father pointed out that my arena of ministry might continue to be writing and publishing, especially to articulate my new spiritual journey which would henceforth color all my future writing. Truly, I have turned a corner that I didn't anticipate and caught a glimpse of a road ahead that I never dreamed of taking.

Father suggested that my recently published autobiography, which I had perceived as "my final word," might be only a launching pad for "the rest of the story" on which I was now embarking. I shared with Father that I had often prayed for God to give me everything He planned for me of spiritual experience and knowledge of Himself. I wanted whatever was in His storehouse with my name on it so that I might faithfully fulfill His will for me "on earth as it is in heaven."

As we discussed the chronological lateness in my life for making what seems like such a drastic change in my Christian faith orientation, he reminded me that Saint Raymond lived to be a hundred years old, and the last phase of his ministry was the most fruitful of his life. That serves as an example to all of us that we are never too old to be instruments of the Lord. The age of the soul has little to do with the age of the body. The ways we can serve the Lord never diminish; they can simply be adjusted and honed to God's continuing purposes for us.

I shared with Father that during the Charismatic spiritual renewal which swept the Christian world in the 1970s, Pastor Jim Brown, a leader of the renewal movement in the

Presbyterian denomination, volunteered a "word of prophecy" for me as he laid hands on me at a prayer service. I kept that declaration to this day on a little card tucked into my Bible. Someone from that church transcribed it verbatim from a tape recording and gave it to me:

"This sister who was baptized as an infant in the Presbyterian church and nurtured and trained in the ways and service of the Lord for many years, shall now bear much fruit for the Kingdom of God in the power of the Holy Spirit. Her training and talents shall now burst into full bloom not only through her natural gifts but through the charisms of the Holy Spirit which will energize her natural gifts. None of her training will be wasted but shall be kindled with power for God's use in a fullness of time that will come in her life. Undreamed of doors shall open to her for ministry for building up the Body of Christ beyond her own or others' imagining. Her lips shall be anointed to speak to people and churches, even large gatherings for the glory of God. Her pen shall be anointed to communicate to this generation the life and power of the Holy Spirit in words they can relate to and many will therefore believe. *The latter season of her life shall be far more fruitful than her former days, thus says the Lord*" (November 1974).

Father said he agreed with this word for me. I accepted his affirmation as a blessing and direction for me in anticipation that God's will might continue to be fulfilled in and through my life in whatever *encrypted* way He chose.

I had a strong sense that *God had His hand on my life* from the beginning to the end.

Chapter 10

WOULD I FLUNK
CONFESSION?

As an evangelical, I never observed Lent, the forty-day period prior to Easter. We learned its significance in RCIA as well as receiving an overview of other rites of the Church that concerned those of us preparing for Confirmation. We studied the seven sacraments, also unfamiliar to me as a Protestant. Since I was baptized as an infant in the Presbyterian Church, the Catholic Church accepted that as a valid baptism and I didn't need to be re-baptized. However, I couldn't provide written proof of my baptism because the little Czech church where I was baptized was no longer standing. No records existed and no one was living who might have witnessed it eighty years ago. In previous years on a visit to Israel I was among several tourists who wanted to be baptized by immersion in the Jordan River at the place where it is believed John baptized Jesus. It was a memorable occasion, and I was able to produce that baptismal certificate which the Catholic Church accepted.

I was still required to go to Confession (the Sacrament of Reconciliation) before Confirmation. We were informed that we didn't have to wait until the entire RCIA group went to Confession the morning of our Confirmation and we could avoid the crowd by going anytime.

On Shrove Tuesday before Ash Wednesday I decided that I wanted to begin observing my first Lenten season by going to my first Confession. I spent many hours, literally days, praying and examining my conscience and listening quietly to the Lord, sometimes in the Adoration Chapel, other times at home. It was a serious, humbling, private experience.

I was so nervous that I was actually afraid I would "flunk Confession"! How could I review my entire long life and still "be brief" as we were instructed? I had been a Christian since my teens and loved and served the Lord all my life. I was fully aware, however, that my life journey was strewn with sins of omission and commission, some known only to me, but all known to God. Yes, I had already repented and confessed those sins privately and directly to God. Yes, I believed God forgave me through the shed blood and sacrifice of Jesus Christ on the cross. Nevertheless, facing what I considered the most significant step of this latter season of my life, I needed to, and finally was willing, even eager to conform to the sacraments of the Catholic Church, That included Confession and absolution. I read widely about that sacrament and knew the seriousness of the practice.

I admit I was scared! This was all so new to me.

As part of our preparation, the previous evening during our RCIA class our leaders took us on a tour of the premises of Sacred Heart Church—every nook and cranny—explaining the breathtaking symbolism, beauty, and sacredness. Our church was ornate with meaningful imagery. Everything was strange to me yet wonderfully sensory, so different from the "plain vanilla" austerity of many of our evangelical churches. For the first time in my life I saw the inside of the Reconciliation rooms at the back of the sanctuary where I would go for Confession.

My only window of opportunity for Confession before Lent would be Tuesday night before Ash Wednesday. I went to church early and spent time in the Adoration Chapel to prepare my heart and gain courage. Then I slipped into a back pew of the sanctuary to wait until it was time for Confession. Suddenly people began arriving and quickly formed two lines leading to the Reconciliation rooms of our two parish priests whose names were on the doors.

I was uncertain which line to join. I stepped arbitrarily into one line, and several people filled in behind me. Most people took only a few minutes for their confession. As we progressed toward the rooms, I whispered to one after another behind me to go ahead of me. I explained that I would probably need a longer session since this was my first Confession. Everyone was so gracious. I received warm hugs from some who assured me they would be praying for me.

The delay also gave me more time to contemplate my cold feet! I could still leave, of course, and put off this encounter with God—but I didn't think God would let me off the hook since I had come this far.

Finally I was the last in line—the caboose. Everyone else had finished and left. I reached the Confessional booth of beloved Father Krempa, our senior priest; I accepted that arrangement as God's will. While my knees shook, I unfolded my three sheets of computer-typed pages that I had labored over in an effort to "be brief and concise" and to remind myself of what I wanted to confess. I wanted to be sure to clear up and clean up all my past transgressions once for all. Having what I wanted to say on paper was my security backup—I was afraid I'd freak out and my mind would go blank if I just tried to wing it.

The red light above the door turns off when a person leaves, and the white light goes on indicating that the next person may step in. It was finally my turn; the door stood open *for me!* The carpeted room was about twice the size of a phone booth with plain walls. There was supposed to be one ceiling light, but I was shocked to see that it must have just burned out. How would I read my notes? There was no chair; a padded kneeling bench faced one wall in which there was a private can't-see-through metal screen. For my anonymity, Father was seated behind the screen in an adjoining little room but not visible to me.

I asked my guardian angel whom I have named Val (for Valiant) to keep me calm and coherent. I asked Saint Michael the Archangel to vanquish Satan and all the prowling mini-devils who might seek to confuse me at this solemn, sacred moment. As soon as I knelt and began to pray the initial liturgical prayer of repentance, a flood of tears hit me and blurred my vision. My composure was shattered!

I couldn't see to read my notes for the dimness of the room and because I dropped some of the sheets while fumbling for a tissue. I was completely unnerved! I would have to try to recall whatever sins the Holy Spirit brought to my mind at the moment. Father remained patiently silent after his first welcoming words and allowed me to sob through all my recitation—perhaps for ten minutes? Maybe only two minutes? I'm not sure; time stood still. Father probably knew who I was; he could recognize my voice.

Father stopped the wild horse's recital of my sins before my final prayer of contrition. He took his time to gently offer me tender counsel, comfort, encouragement, and common-sense direction in a warm, fatherly way. That just brought on another flood of tears of relief and loud blowing of my nose causing me to drop the remainder of my notes on the floor.

I wept through my liturgical prayer of contrition and my declaration of intent to avoid further occasions of sin and to pursue a holy life with the help of God. The penance Father Krempa gave me was to meditate on certain Scripture passages in the gospels when I left the Confessional. Then he quietly pronounced absolution for my sins, *in persona Christi* (acting in the person of Christ) by virtue of his anointed office as a priest. I understood that when a priest enters the Confessional, he "puts on Christ" as it were. It is not the priest who forgives my sins, of course, but it is Christ. His words penetrated the depths of my heart as I acknowledged his biblical authority to declare that Jesus forgave my sins.

I gathered up my notes from the floor and stumbled out of the Reconciliation room. I felt humbled, deeply repentant, remorseful, yet joyful and relieved—all at the same time. I was grateful for the generous mercy, patience, and love of God who Himself lifted my guilt and cleansed me from all my past sins. I was thankful for God's tremendous mercy, which I felt unworthy to receive, in not exposing me publicly for private sins in my past. I felt fresh and renewed, restored to the joy of my salvation and eager to embark on an even closer relationship with Jesus than ever before.

Many times I had experienced deep repentance for my sins. I knew God forgave me according to the promises in Scripture. Nevertheless, the feeling of guilt somehow lingered. I could more easily forgive others their transgressions against me than forgive myself for having transgressed and fallen short of what pleased God. To hear with my own ears the words of absolution was overwhelming and relieving.

Because I was still awash with tears, I slipped into the back pew of the quiet, now nearly deserted sanctuary. I knelt praying until I could regain control of my emotions. I fixed my eyes on the large carved crucifix that hung high above the altar illumined by a soft spotlight in the dim light of this beautiful church. I whispered the responsorial declaration we recite at Mass: *"Christ has died; Christ has risen; Christ will come again."* My heart burned within me with the desire to live henceforth in a state of grace. I wanted to pursue holiness and love the Lord with all my heart and soul and mind because my offenses had first of all been against Him. I read the gospel portions Father Krempa had instructed me to meditate on.

As I left the sanctuary, I saw Jeff Zirkle, my precious good buddy and RCIA sponsor for my Confirmation, waiting to give me a big hug. Echoing the commercial slogan of some years ago, he grinned, "You've come a long way, baby!" (Yes, I was like a baby, learning all the first steps not of a new walk but a renewed walk with Christ in the company of new brothers and sisters in Christ.)

A convert from Protestantism himself, this man of God was my support from the start of my critical exploration of the Catholic faith. He knew that the Sacrament of Reconciliation had loomed as a big hurdle for me because my evangelical habit was to confess to Jesus exclusively—certainly not to a mortal man or even through one. Of course, I can and will continue to confess my transgressions to Jesus directly, but the Scriptures clearly record that Jesus instructed His Church through the ages how to deal with the need to confess sin and receive forgiveness (John 20:22-23; Matt. 18:18; James 5:13-15).

As an evangelical, I was inclined to think of repentance more or less as an initial and one time act and acknowledgment that "all have sinned and come short of the glory of God," and so have I. It was something one did at the time of praying to accept Jesus as one's personal Savior. My further careful study of Scripture, the Gospels, and the record of the early Church convinced me that the mandate and authority to forgive post-baptismal sins was clearly given by Jesus to the apostles who passed it on to anointed successors through the apostolic Church. God gave me the firm faith to embrace this biblical sacrament as a desirable and welcome opportunity established by Jesus for mercy, cleansing, restoration and healing available on a continuing basis to His needy children.

I made my way out through the narthex and the cloistered arches to the parking lot of the church. I looked up at the dark night sky and wondered whether my first Confession had caused a joyful ruckus among the angel hosts in heaven at the sight of this repentant sinner, according to the words of Jesus in Luke 15:7.

I drove home in my Chrysler, but I felt as if I could have floated through the air on the joy of God's forgiveness.

Chapter 11

COMING HOME

After my first Confession, throughout the night and into the next morning I was on the verge of joyful tears; I was experiencing an emotional and spiritual high. The following day was Ash Wednesday, the beginning of Lent. For the first time I received the mark of the cross with ashes on my forehead as a sobering reminder of our human mortality.

As I progressed toward Easter I felt more prepared now for deeper lessons of faith and sacrifice. Psalm 51 came alive as I prayed with King David in the personal pronouns he expressed in his repentance, confession, and restoration. My contrition during the Sacrament of Reconciliation echoed David's. I wanted to keep living with a tender heart that kept my tears close to the surface, tears celebrating God's mercy and forgiveness. The antiphon for that day at Mass from Joel, Chapter 2 was full of meaning for me:

Come back to the Lord with all your heart;
Leave the past in ashes,
And turn to God with tears and fasting,
for he is slow to anger and ready to forgive.

And from the Responsorial, "Direct our hearts to better things, O Lord; heal our sin and ignorance." I needed that kind of healing as I moved toward my Confirmation.

I wanted some sensory and symbolic action to illustrate my determination to *"leave the past in ashes."* I took the three typed sheets of lifetime sins I had prepared for my confession, a box of matches, a cone of incense, and a small glass jar to the driveway beside the little chalet in the woods where I lived at the time. I shredded the paper into a pile on the gravel, tucked the incense cone into it, and lit a match. I made the sign of the cross as I silently knelt to watch the little pile blaze and burn within a few minutes to gray ashes while the fragrance of incense rose toward heaven. Tears again.

I prayed, "Have mercy on me, O God, in your goodness; in the greatness of your compassion wipe out my offense. Thoroughly wash me from my guilt and of my sin cleanse me" (Psalm 51:1-2).

I scooped into the little jar what was left of the paper ash and screwed on the lid. I will keep it to remind me that "Not according to our sins does he deal with us, nor does he requite us according to our crimes... As far as the east is from the west, so far has he put our transgressions from us" (Psalm 103:10, 12)

Coming Home

Through a series of Rites during several Sunday Masses, as catechumens and candidates we moved toward Confirmation by being publicly introduced to the congregation. Father Krempa, designated by our bishop to celebrate the Rites, called us forward to bless us individually. The prayer and charge by Ed, one of our RCIA leaders, commended us to the prayers of the faithful people of the parish as we progressed to the "finish line" at Easter Vigil. Our Confirmation was, however, more like a "starting gun" to live a renewed Christian life for whatever span of life lay ahead of each of us.

During most of my journey into the Church, I wrestled intellectually with theological matters. Since I finally settled that struggle, and after my first Confession, the spiritual and emotional aspects came to the forefront. The concluding hymn at the Mass was "Hosea," probably familiar to the Catholic congregation but not to this evangelical. Its soulful strains and meaningful lyrics brought on fresh tears as I knelt:

Come back to me with all your heart.
Don't let fear keep us apart.
Trees do bend though straight and tall;
so must we to others' call.
Long have I waited for your coming home to me
and living deeply our new life.

My RCIA friend, Sandra, sitting beside me, offered her folded white handkerchief, which she told me later to keep. It was her "tears at Mass" hankie, always clean and available. Another sweet, very young RCIA friend, Elizabeth, who knelt at my left, shared my deep feelings and accepted tissues from me.

I prayed, "Lord, have You really waited a long time for me to come Home? You are Eternal so it was probably just a brief moment for You. For me it was nearly 80 years—the age of Moses when You called him in the wilderness to what seemed like an impossible task.

"Lord, I have come Home!

"In retrospect, I understand that my Trinitarian baptism as an infant was my Rite of Election, my entry into the household of Christ. I understand now why I sought You early in life without anyone giving me formal instruction in the faith. Although I can't point to a day or hour when I "accepted You into my heart," it seems that I always wanted You, Jesus. I accepted all of You that my child heart could hold. Purely by Your grace, my heart was inclined toward You and receptive to Your generous love.

"I sense that You chose me from before the foundation of the world, as the Scripture declares, to be Your own child, and that You appointed the details of my earthly life journey. I pressed on to Your deeper truths—Your higher callings, more light, more Living Water, more depth of Your riches and more fire of the Holy Spirit's power for my weakness. Thank You for Your boundless mercy and lavish love!"

I have already been "home" in the satisfied sense of being in Jesus' sheepfold from my early youth. So how can I explain what has happened at this final season of my life? Why do I say that I have "finally come Home"?

For the most part, I was not a prodigal wasting the goodness of God on riotous living far from home. Although I failed many times, I sincerely tried to follow the light of truth as I understood it among the various Protestant branches of the Christian tree. That was all that I knew, and I believe God was pleased with my desire to be faithful.

By the goodness and mercy of God and His penchant for late-in-life surprises, He drew me Home from the living branches of the tree to embrace the trunk of the Christian tree—the one, holy, Catholic, and apostolic Church. Through the sovereign move of God in my life when I least expected it, I have come Home. It has been a long journey; but I am ready to *"live our new life deeply…with all my heart."* Although life on the branches was good, life in the trunk is fullness with its taproot deep in the apostolic faith.

"Trees do bend, though straight and tall…." I've sincerely tried

throughout my life to be "straight and tall" in my evangelical faith and its practice. I confess, however, that my shortcomings, omissions and failures have been significant. "Lord, be merciful to me, a sinner."

To take this step I must bend. I must bow in humility. I express this every time I lower my knees to the kneelers at Mass, something to which I was not accustomed as an evangelical. It is symbolic yet more than symbolic; it effects what it signifies. I will bend to make this gesture of my surrender to the fullness of God's Truth as I have now found it.

I had a litany of fears when I contemplated this drastic step: fear for my Christian reputation, fear of how family, friends, and co-workers would perceive my decision and criticize me. Fear of losing lifelong friends and not being able to make new ones. Fear of disappointing, even disillusioning, those I love. Fear that I might not be able to endure the ramifications of this change in the long haul. Fear that I won't be able to explain my decision adequately. Fear of the strangeness of the new Catholic Christian culture into which I am stepping.

Most of those fears were based on my pride and lack of complete trust in God's leading. I should fear instead to disobey the new light which God is giving me.

The tender voice of God came through the hymn that so touched my heart, "*Don't let fear keep us apart.*"

Rather than focusing on my fears, I rejoice in how honored I feel that God would so surprisingly work in my life in my latter years to bring me into still greater fullness of His Truth—step by step toward Home. I have a strong sense of having been chosen from the day I was baptized as an infant. So how could I refuse to trust God and eagerly "*live deeply our new life*"? I shall "give no thought to what lies behind but push on to what is ahead. My entire attention is on the finish line as I run toward the prize to which God calls me—life on high in Christ Jesus" (Philippians 3:13-14).

My Patron Saint

As our RCIA class neared Confirmation, our leaders asked us to prayerfully choose a patron saint who might have some relevance to our new lives as Catholics. I knew immediately that mine would be Saint Francis de Sales, a bishop and Doctor of the Church who died in 1622. I had never heard of him while I was an evangelical. He is the patron saint of writers and those in media.

Not incidental to my choice was that my father's name was Frank (Francis), Frantisek in Czech; my paternal grandmother's name was Frantiska or Frances; and my middle name is Frances. As I read the saint's famous book, *An Introduction to the Devout Life*, the depth and style of his writing resonated in my spirit.

A thoughtful RCIA friend gave me a laminated card with a picture, quotation, and a prayer of Francis de Sales which I am attempting to internalize:

"Do not look forward to what may happen tomorrow; the same everlasting Father who cares for you today will take care of you tomorrow and every day. Either He will shield you from suffering, or He will give you unfailing strength to bear it. Be at peace, then. Put aside all anxious thoughts and imaginations, and say continually: 'The Lord is my strength and my shield; my heart has trusted in Him and I am helped. He is not only with me, but in me and I in Him.'

"Most loving and lovable Saint, you preached to thousands with the pen, introducing them to 'the devout life.' You wrote sublimely about God's love and made countless converts by your Christ-like kindness. Cause writers to realize the power of the Press and inspire them with your zeal for spreading truth. Help them write honestly no matter what the subject, so that they will really contribute to bringing about God's Kingdom."

In the infancy of my Catholic faith, and in my own naiveté, I had no idea how much my current step of faith would affect my creative writing and publishing. I was yet to realize those implications when I began to flesh out my adjusted biblical beliefs after I was received into the Church. I would need the intercession of Saint Francis de Sales for my writing more than I could have imagined!

Strength for the Journey

In our RCIA class I learned about still another sacrament on my journey Home which I could request and whose wonderful graces I could experience.

Was I so greedy? No, perhaps I was covetous in a positive sense. I was hungry and thirsty for everything offered at the banquet table of the Catholic Church which is spread with a bounty of healthful spiritual nourishment. I received an engraved invitation from God, so to speak, to "Come and dine" around a new family table where I now would belong. The large leather "menu" had Seven Entrees. I experienced the once-for-all Sacrament of Baptism as an infant; my first Confession had been another sacrament. At Easter Vigil I would experience two more, Confirmation and the Eucharist.

I didn't think the sacraments of Matrimony and Holy Orders were available to me at this late point in my life! Nevertheless, I recognize that I do have Holy Orders in some sense—the Church teaches that the universal call to holiness is truly for each of us. My orders from God are that I should become increasingly more holy. Matrimony? I am truly moving toward union with Christ.

I believe it is in accord with the teachings of the Catholic Church and pleasing to God to want more graces and blessings so I could be well nourished spiritually. I didn't want to indulge myself selfishly, but to be available for God to channel graces through me for the benefit of others.

Therefore, I requested the seventh sacrament, the Sacrament of Anointing for healing.

Was I ill? Not at the moment. But then I read in our RCIA text, "The sick person need not be in danger of death. For example, an elderly person who is in a weakened condition may be anointed even though no specific serious illness is present."

I wondered whether I would be eligible. I'll reach eighty this year. I'm a thankful survivor of lung cancer surgery. I would like to ask God for continued strength to fulfill His remaining purposes through me.

Our parish priest assured me I qualified for that sacrament!

I guess it's time to start admitting that I am "elderly," but because I have Eternal Life through Jesus Christ, I haven't considered chronological age a significant factor. I hope to continue "mounting up with wings as an eagle" (Psalm 40) and living out the promise of Psalm 103 that "your youth is renewed like the eagle's." God promises "with length of days I will gratify him and will show him my salvation" (Psalm 91).

"Thank You, Lord, for the long life You have already generously granted me. I have lived to see my children grown, and my children's children, and great-grandchildren. If it is not too much to ask and in Your perfect will, I request still more time to live for You and serve You. I need strength for the rest of this journey on earth before I leave to rejoice in Your eternal presence."

From the promises of Psalm 92, I see that it is God's plan for the elderly to be righteous and to "flourish like the palm tree, like a cedar of Lebanon shall he grow... and flourish in the courts of our God. They shall bear fruit even in old age; vigorous and sturdy shall they be...." "I want to be like that for You, Lord."

I flipped the pages of the Catechism for further teaching on that sacrament so I could prepare myself for such a serious event. The teaching was based in part on verses in the letter of James, Chapter 5. The initiative to receive the sacrament was supposed to come from the one desiring its graces.

Okay, so I fulfilled that by requesting it from our parochial vicar, the late Father Michael Craig Kelly. He agreed to administer the sacrament on the following day which, not by coincidence, was the *World Day of Prayer for the Sick* as declared by Pope John Paul II. I had recently read the Pope's "Letter to the Elderly" which set a high and holy standard for continuing a productive life in Christ in one's advancing years.

In the Catechism I read, "When anyone of the faithful begins to be in danger of death from sickness or old age, the fitting time for him to receive this sacrament has certainly already arrived." Yes, I see most of my life in the rearview mirror.

I was further assured, "The same holds for the elderly whose frailty becomes more pronounced." Yes, again. I am in the age bracket of those who certainly do feel increasing weakness and growing limitations. I would welcome the physical, mental, and spiritual nourishment of this sacrament to shore me up.

"It is to be preceded by the Sacrament of Penance if possible." I had just experienced my first Reconciliation and was reveling in the mercy of God, the forgiveness of sins, and the joy of absolution.

What wonderful graces and effects could I expect from this sacrament? Again the Catechism spelled out the promises. It was like a table prepared in the wilderness of life for a festive meal!

"The first grace of this sacrament is one of strengthening, peace, and courage to overcome the difficulties that go with the condition of serious illness or the frailty of old age. This grace is a gift of the Holy Spirit, who renews trust and faith in God and strengthens against the temptations of the evil one, the temptation to discouragement and anguish in the face of death. This assistance from the Lord by the power of his Spirit is meant to lead the sick [or elderly] person to healing of the soul, but also of the body if such is God's will. Furthermore, 'if he has committed sins, he will be forgiven.'"

Yes! I want to receive it all. I need an overhaul of renewal for strength, trust, and faith to meet the potential discouragements and temptations along the rest of my earthly journey.

A further benefit? "By the grace of this sacrament the sick [or elderly] person receives the strength and the gift of uniting himself more closely to Christ's Passion: in a certain way he is consecrated to bear fruit by configuration to the Savior's redemptive Passion. Suffering, a consequence of original sin, acquires a new meaning; it becomes a participation in the saving work of Jesus."

Yes! I desire that. How appropriate that we are beginning the Lenten season and my heart and mind are focused in a new way on Christ's Passion and Resurrection!

And still more benefit! "The sick [elderly], who receive this sacrament, 'by freely uniting themselves to the passion and death of Christ, contribute to the good of the People of God.' By celebrating this sacrament, the Church, in the communion of saints, intercedes for the benefit of the sick [elderly] person, and he, for his part, through the grace of this sacrament, contributes to the sanctification of the Church and to the good of all men for whom the Church suffers and offers herself through Christ to God the Father."

Yes again! I don't fully understand what this is all about; I am still a kindergarten Catholic, not even confirmed. Nevertheless, I trust the authoritative teaching of the Church. I accept this by faith. I want strength, the maintenance of my health and, if God wills, the extension of my life, not for myself alone but to benefit the entire Body of Christ, the Church, in whatever way God may dispense it.

This sacrament is "to be received with good disposition." I examined my heart for purity of motive. I asked the Lord to increase my faith so that the act of anointing by the priest, his words spoken over me, and my heart response would make the sacrament efficacious.

I eagerly anticipated receiving the sacrament that night. "Let it be done unto me according to Thy word."

A few parishioners were already seated in the sanctuary or kneeling in silence although it was still a half hour before the Stations of the Cross would begin. Father Kelly was waiting for me and he motioned that we should walk together down the aisle to a front pew where I knelt facing him and toward the altar. He put his priestly stole across his shoulders and began to read the beautiful liturgy of the sacrament, indicating to me at intervals what my response should be to his readings from the Scriptures and to his prayers.

When he concluded, he placed his hands on my head and held them there as he prayed silently. Then he anointed my forehead and the top of both my hands with holy oil and prayed for blessings upon me for the future according to my needs and the promises of God.

"I have been anointed with rich oil" (Psalm 92). "You anoint my head with oil; my cup overflows" (Psalm 23).

We recited the Our Father together, made the sign of the cross, and Father prayed a final blessing upon me.

After genuflecting toward the tabernacle, we both walked back up the aisle. I took my seat in the pew by my waiting friend, and she and I knelt in silent prayer to prepare our hearts for the Stations of the Cross.

Without fanfare and with deep meaning, I had quietly met with God and received His blessing through His servant, Father Kelly, for spiritual and physical sustenance for the rest of my life's way. I pray that in my remaining time on earth I may become more holy and more worthy of God's surprising new grace to me. Until recently I thought there was "nothing beyond" what I had already learned, taught and experienced in my evangelical Christian life, ministry, and missionary service.

Before Columbus sailed to America, the coat of arms of Spain carried the motto *Ne Plus Ultra*, which means, "There is nothing beyond." But Columbus burned with a vision of undiscovered lands beyond the ocean's horizon where people lived who needed the Christian message. He bravely risked the terrors of the unknown and uncharted seas of that time. After his discoveries of the new world and new peoples, the *Ne* was dropped from the coat of arms leaving *Plus Ultra*—There is MORE beyond!

I, too, am discovering immeasurably MORE in the one, holy, Catholic, and apostolic Church.

In this latter season of my life, God beckons me to launch out into the unknown deep once more. Perhaps there is a great draught of fishes out there somewhere. I must eagerly press on to follow the Lord. *"Close to Thee, Lord, I shall sail other seas!"* They were previously unexplored and unknown to me—but they were already charted by Him.

Since God is investing such generous blessings in me, I want to bring forth fruit, more fruit, and much sweet fruit for His glory. Only as I abide in Jesus can the fruit and the gifts of the Holy Spirit come forth in fullness.

So may it be. God has His hand on my life.

Chapter 12

COLD FEET OR WET FEET?

Line in the Sand—or in Cement?

It was a week before Easter Vigil and my scheduled Confirmation. I was experiencing virtual before-the-wedding jitters. We were told in our RCIA class that when we made our profession of faith, we would declare: "I believe and profess all that the holy Catholic Church believes, teaches, and proclaims to be revealed by God."

So—what else would I expect? Why does this shake me up at almost the last minute? A bride should be eager to say "I do" and surrender herself entirely to her beloved and look forward joyfully to all that the married state will hold. "Obey" is sometimes omitted from wedding vows these days, but it is nevertheless implied. The promises the couple makes are supposed to express an irrevocable, unconditional, comprehensive commitment.

Likewise, this spiritual commitment is binding and inclusive and deliberately made in public.

Suddenly I am shaky. I'm not trying an evasive tactic, but I start to question the definition of "all." I certainly don't understand all that the Catholic Church teaches. I don't know it all. Which Catholic teachings are mandatory/obligatory to believe and which are optional? Are any of them optional? I've met a number of "cafeteria Catholics" who pick and choose what they accept or practice. I don't want to go there. That confuses me. I also read that certain things are left up to an individual's conscience, that some practices are not dogmas or doctrines but disciplines or regulations or customs that can actually change with the times.

I really am not asking how little I can believe and still be Catholic, but I sincerely would like to clarify my declaration of faith. It is too serious for mere lip service.

I don't want to be a cafeteria Catholic. If I am going to pick and choose, I might as well stay a Protestant. I am becoming a Catholic because I diligently sought the truth, the whole truth, and nothing but the truth. Since I found it, I could never turn back! I can no longer be a Protestant because I could not protest against the one, holy, Catholic, and apostolic church. I know too much Catholic truth to retreat with integrity. The dogmatic truth that squared with the Bible was what drew me to the Church. There was nothing wishy-washy about it.

Why then do I feel such inner pressure and uncertainty right now as I stand on the edge of the diving board? My stress level is high; suddenly I'm not as happy a camper as I ought to be as I approach my Confirmation. What's the matter with me?

Am I not sure that *God has His hand on my life?*

I shook myself to sobriety and answered my own question. The devil is a joy robber. He must be taking a last-ditch swipe at my decision. He tried many of his wiles to discourage me by both theological and personal attacks through people who are close to me. Although criticism and misunderstanding come from people, Satan is behind the scenes. We wrestle not against flesh and blood but against invisible, evil, spiritual powers (Ephesians 6).

There are times when the devil still whispers in my ear; he just won't give up: How in the world do you dare do what you are doing after a lifetime of Protestant ministry? Your decision is affecting so many people adversely. What a responsibility you bear! You have been brainwashed by gradually exposing yourself to the Catholic side of history and theology. You are like the frog immersed in cold water that was gradually heated to the boiling point. You got cooked in it! Besides, it is too late in life for you to make such a shift in your faith. Change is too hard. Take the easy way—go back to your *status quo*. You don't have to go through with this. They said you could even change your mind at the last minute....

Help! Help! Lord, I'm about to sink after trying to walk on the water. God, come to my assistance; Lord, make haste to help me!

Scripture instructs me to tell the devil to go where he belongs. I am to command him to flee, to cease and desist. I DO SO! Lord, lead us not into temptation, but deliver us from evil."

My problem comes when I try to run on my feelings and not on faith. I know better. I know God will always be faithful when I ask Him to keep me from going astray. He wouldn't deceive me or let me be deceived by error and false teaching. I am a sheep who has been trained over a lifetime to hear the voice of my Shepherd. Surely He would have stopped me before this, if I were making a mistake. I am simply going through the normal cold-feet phase a bride experiences before she walks down the aisle.

Surprisingly, John the Baptist questioned whether Jesus was truly the prophesied Messiah even after he initially announced him as such. Jesus didn't rebuke him for questioning but reassured him. Neither do I want to be "a reed shaken by the wind." Lord, I confess my unfounded doubts and questions. "I believe! Lord, help my unbelief.... Only say the word and I shall be healed."

Yes, truly, *God has His hand on my life!*

I hereby surrender to Truth, to the Church which Jesus established as His Body, His Bride. I surrender my own opinions. I surrender my past misunderstandings, and incomplete beliefs. I embrace Jesus wholly in His Church. I exchange my previous partial light for full light.

In all sincerity I asked God to reveal His fullness of Truth, to give me all the graces He has in store for me while I am on earth. I believe He is giving me that fullness in the Catholic Church. I hereby exercise my free will by choosing once for all to surrender my will to the authority that God ordained.

I put my hand to the plow, and I will not look back. This is my line in the sand. No—a line in the sand can still be washed away or altered. I draw my line in wet cement! It is irrevocable.

My Czech ancestors crossed not the Tiber but the Atlantic Ocean to make the long, dangerous voyage to the promised land of America. Halfway across they may have asked one another, "What are we thinking? We are risking everything! We can't even speak English! We've never seen America! We don't know the customs, we have no skills, and we are without resources. Our decision will affect all of our descendants for generations to come!"

Living in America was no picnic for these immigrants. Nevertheless, they learned the language, worked hard, bought land, educated their children, endured hardships, and the strange land became "home." They were living in the land of more—more than they had ever imagined. They never seriously doubted whether their decision had been good, especially when Hitler's cruel armies swept over their Czech homeland followed soon afterward by Russian troops who ravaged their land and enslaved the people.

In a similar sense, I am entering an unfamiliar land of promise and a different religious culture and sacred Christian tradition with some of the same challenges as my immigrant ancestors. However, I do have unlimited resources in Jesus Christ whom I have trusted for a lifetime and continue to trust. He is the same yesterday, today, yes and forever (Hebrews 13:8). He has abundant graces prepared for me. I am willing to take responsibility under God to change the direction of the destiny of my descendants beyond my lifetime, if God wills. I accept that mandate.

May God forgive me for my shaking knees and pity party on the verge of crossing into the wonderful *Land of More*. It has been spiritually, intellectually, and emotionally traumatic to make such a quantum religious leap. The cost is high, but the cost is a pittance compared to what it cost my Lord to obtain my salvation through His suffering and death on the cross. I won't draw back like the ten fearful spies returning from the land of Canaan with a report of incredible abundance but overwhelmed with the difficulties and their own inadequacy. I will emulate courageous Caleb and Joshua.

I know *God has His hand on my life!*

I won't focus on my detractors and critics; instead I will humbly thank God for the guides, mentors, spiritual instructors, Bible teachers, and new praying friends who cheer me on and help me safely cross this sacred threshold. They are God-sent flesh and blood angels who are upholding me through my struggles to joyful victory.

I want it all—all the graces that God has in store for me through Himself and His Church and His people in *The Land of More*.

I renew my baptismal promises. When I was immersed in the Jordan River the water was deep. I don't want to stay in the shallows spiritually. I long to experience more of God's depths. I ask for an outpouring of His rain from heaven. I invite the fire of the Holy Spirit to empower me to live the new life that lies ahead.

Fiat! Let it be done unto me according to His word.

WET FEET *

How can I say
I experience The Ocean
when only my feet get wet?

Sand between my toes
I slosh around in the
     shallows.
Have I no regret
that I haven't tasted yet
God's Midstream Ecstasy
with the pull of its current
crashing waves
and deep euphoria?

Is shallow safe?
Is superficial satisfying?
Is deep dangerous?
Oh! the false premises
     embraced
by humdrum humanity!

I could miss
The Great Everything
by bartering it
for little nothings
safe sedatives
that chain me to the shore
eroding, consuming
my hours, days, and years.

Are the shallows risk free?
Probably
but with a phony guarantee
that lulls me
into insensitivity
and deceptive security
as I wade only ankle deep
in The Fathomless Ocean
of His Abundant Life.
Take me to the deep, Lord!
Immerse me totally!

RAIN ON ME *

I hear the whisper
of abundance of Rain
in the restless tree tops
I smell it in the air
feel it damp against my face
all earth is hushed
as the distant rumble of
    thunder
heralds the refreshment to
    come:
Rain on me, Lord!

I stand vulnerable
bare skin longing
dry spirit crying
empty hands spread
soul thirsting:
Rain on me!

Drench me
soak me
saturate me
with the Rain of heaven
not just "mercy drops"
nor "raindrops fallin' on my
    head"
not a drizzle or a sprinkle
but for the showers I plead:
Rain on me!

Parched ground cracks
withered foliage droops
creatures moan from thirst
with all creation I cry:
Rain on me!

Inundate me
let Your clouds burst above
let the heavens open
let the lightning crash:
Rain on me!

Let the water rise around me
let me plant my feet
in Your flooded river
hands and face uplifted
take me to the Depths, Lord
wash Your waves over me
propel me wherever
Your swift current
wills to carry my soul
toward the destiny
You've ordained for me:
Keep raining on me!

Do I want an umbrella?
NO, SATAN, NO!

FRESH FIRE *

Veni Sancte Spiritus
Come, Holy Spirit
descend on me with FRESH FIRE
flames of Pentecost, tongues of FIRE
fall upon and fill me
renew my stony heart to flesh
purify my soul
burn away the dross of self.

O Holy Spirit of God
Light Your Church AFIRE
transform us to burning bushes
living sacrifices yet not consumed
touch our lips with glowing coals until
we are fully possessed by You
to speak holy words, think holy thoughts.

We see reflected in Your holy FIRE
the brilliance of Your Manifest Presence
let the flames of Your searing love
blaze fiercely on the altars of our hearts
never quenched, never diminished
a perpetual sacrifice of praise
as fragrant incense rising to Your throne.

O Spirit, impart to me a burning heart
as I walk with Christ on my Emmaus road
fan the embers of my passion
back to "first love" intensity.

140

O Spirit, endue Your Church with holy power
to spread Your FIRE abroad
and ignite the Final Harvest fields ablaze
to rescue rebellious mankind
from the kingdom of darkness
to Your brilliant Kingdom of Light
by Your uncommon FIRE!

* Poetry by the author

Chapter 13

THIS IS THE DAY!

After a nearly four-year journey of inquiry into the Catholic faith, and after a lifetime Christian faith journey, this was finally the day and the very hour I was to be received into the Catholic Church.

And I almost missed it!

But God's hand was on my life.

Sacred Heart of Jesus Catholic Church in Winchester, Virginia was packed on the evening of Easter Vigil March 2005. Lilies and other flowers in full bloom exploded their fragrance and beauty throughout the sanctuary. I could hardly believe it—twenty-four of my supporting friends and family were seated in reserved pews with me! The group included all four of my adult sons. I was deeply moved at this warm expression of their love and support. One of my sons surprised me by saying, in effect, "I'm proud of your courage. Go for it, Mom!"

My RCIA sponsor and parish mentor, Jeff, sat beside me. Both of my long- distance spiritual mentors were present. Rod Bennett drove from Georgia with his daughter, and Dr. Robin Maas with her husband Jack came from northern Virginia. Mary Catherine, another mentor from the parish who was assigned to me by RCIA, was in the choir. (I guess it took four mentors because I was such a difficult case!) A friend I had not previously met drove from Tennessee, and other friends arrived from Maryland and West Virginia. All were present to witness this earthquake step in my life.

Conspicuously absent were some of my closest evangelical Christian friends who simply couldn't support what they considered a spiritually disappointing step backward for me.

Ushers handed a candle to each person entering the sanctuary in preparation for the Service of Light. At 8:30 the lights in the church were turned off; we sat in total darkness. Following the Easter tradition, a new fire was kindled outside the sanctuary and from it the tall, new Easter candle was lit. Other symbolic rites followed with singing. Our priest chanted, "May the light of Christ rising in glory dispel the darkness of our hearts and minds." The procession began to the accompaniment of the choir in the balcony at the rear. Several priests in white and gold vestments, white-robed young acolytes holding candles aloft, and Knights of Columbus men in formal regalia wearing feather-plumed hats with swords at their sides marched down the center aisle. Deacon Ed, the leader of the procession, held the Easter candle high.

Each person in the pews lit his candle from the candle of the person beside him, the first candle on the aisle being lit from the Easter candle. Gradually the darkness gave way to the stunning brilliance of hundreds of candles. Then all the lights in the church were switched back on—a spectacular ceremony began!

And I almost missed it!

The Easter Proclamation (*Exsultet*) was recited responsively concluding with triumphantly singing, "May the Morning Star which never sets find this flame still burning; Christ, that Morning Star, who came back from the dead, and shed his peaceful light on all mankind, your Son who lives and reigns forever and ever. Amen."

Several lengthy portions of Scripture from the Old Testament, the Epistles, and the Gospels were presented by different lay readers. The selections recalled how God guided and saved his people throughout biblical history, and in the fullness of time sent his own Son to be our Redeemer. The priest chanted a psalm to which the people responded in a refrain, and various liturgical prayers followed. After the last reading, the altar servers lit the remaining many candles on the altar, and the congregation joined in singing a jubilant *Gloria*. At its conclusion, all the church bells inside and outside rang out loudly in celebration of Christ raised from the dead to die no more.

And I almost missed it!

Those of our RCIA group who had not been baptized went forward with their godparents for the liturgy that accompanied the Sacrament of Baptism. The font had been brought from its usual place in the narthex and placed at the front near the altar.

Our priests led the Litany of the Saints with response by the congregation followed by the long-awaited Confirmation ceremony. As each of our names was called we went forward. Our sponsors stood behind us, hand on our shoulder, holding a card with the name of the patron saint each of us had chosen. We were asked individually to assent to our profession of faith:

"I believe and profess all that the holy Catholic Church believes, teaches, and proclaims to be revealed by God."

There it was—I put my hand to the plow without looking back!

The priest took his time to lay hands on each of our heads

in turn, pray, and anoint our foreheads with holy oil. I heard, "Leona, the Lord receives you into the Catholic Church. His loving kindness has led you here, so that in the unity of the Holy Spirit you may have full communion with us in the faith that you have professed in the presence of his family."

The congregation stood with us holding lighted candles. All were asked to renew our baptismal promises—to reject Satan and all his works, his empty promises, and all sin. We responded, "I do." In unison we affirmed the declarations of the Apostles' Creed.

After we took our seats, Father Krempa exuberantly processed up and down the aisles sprinkling the people with a hyssop branch dipped in holy water. (We were advised beforehand to remove our glasses if we didn't want our "windshields" splashed!)

And I almost missed this ceremony!

The Liturgy of the Eucharist followed. We who were being received into the Church were the first to receive the wine and the bread. Although I anticipated feeling overwhelmed with emotion during this faith milestone in my life, it all passed too quickly in a blur. A kind of supernatural peace and calmness settled upon me like a cloud. I felt an aura of unreality, as if I were a spectator looking on the scene.

I wanted to seize the moment and hold it fast. I was excited to realize, however, that this wonderful moment of experiencing the Sacrament of the Eucharist was not only continually repeatable and daily available, but that it would become even more precious as time went by and equally efficacious each time I received it. It was not merely a symbol; it was the real presence of Jesus Christ. I partook of His very Body and Blood (John 6).

God daily prepares a table before me (Psalm 23) and knocks every day at my heart's door asking to come in and eat with me and I with Him (Revelation 3:20). Jesus teaches me in His "Our Father" prayer to ask for "my daily bread." The Sacrament of the Eucharist carries with it the forgiveness of sins, healing, the anointing of the love of God, spiritual empowering, and union with His entire Body in Heaven and on earth.

And I almost missed it!

WHY have I repeatedly said that I almost missed it?

An Invisible Battle Raging

Satan had been trying in every way to attack me, to deter me, to discourage me, to bring doubts, and to hold back my decision. He used all his wiles to stop me from publicly renouncing him and surrendering totally to God the Father, Son, and Holy Spirit and being received into the Church which Christ established. He was unrelenting, persisting to the very limit of his limited yet powerful spiritual warfare.

After my long journey Home to Mother Catholic Church, a journey I would never have dreamed of making in the first place, I was finally joyfully confident to accept the fullness of all the Church stood for. Satan was obviously losing his battle against me.

Still not giving up, the devil turned up the heat. During the last few weeks before the Easter Vigil he intensified his opposition. He used the criticism of people, theological disputations, misunderstandings, sticky circumstances, distractions to my mind, multiplied concerns of this world—but none succeeded. I had supernatural defense and protection from on high. Greater was He who was in me than he who was in the world—the prince of darkness.

147

The devil tried a last-ditch strategy—he attacked my body. The week before the Easter Vigil I suddenly experienced a whopper of an allergy attack with sneezing, coughing, and congestion that made me feel absolutely wretched. No medication, including allergy shots, relieved it.

On the heels of that, I picked up a vicious virus that sapped my energy and increased my feeling of despair. The doctor said no medication would help and that I'd simply have to let it run its course—and the course might be a long one.

Painful sinusitis was thrown into the mix, and the virus settled in my right eye causing it to be red, swollen, watery, sore, and half-closed with discharge. The ophthalmologist prescribed antibiotic drops but cautioned that by tomorrow (Easter Vigil) it would probably spread to the other eye. There was no quick fix.

All I wanted to do was crawl into bed, pull up the covers, and sleep until after Easter. But then I would miss my Confirmation and the devil would have the last laugh! Some of my formerly good friends who now opposed me might take it as a sign that God was stopping me from embracing heresy!

Lord, have mercy!

I called upon Jesus to help me.

God had His hand on my life!

Water into Wine

I shared my desperate physical infirmity with precious, faithful, new Catholic prayer partners locally and across the country. They in turn phoned or e-mailed other intercessors. I asked Michael the Archangel to step up his protection and call on his angelic reinforcements if necessary. I pleaded with my guardian angel, Valiant, to rescue me. I asked all the departed saints with whom I had become acquainted in the Communion of Saints to pray to Jesus for me; I likewise entreated my alive-in-heaven family and friends. I asked for the intercession of my patron saint, Francis de Sales, patron of writers, whose name I would take at Confirmation.

Yes, I called upon the Blessed Virgin Mary, whom I didn't know very well yet. My spiritual mentor, Dr. Maas, recommended that I daily ask Jesus, "If it is Your will and desire that Your Mother be an important part of my growth in holiness, please find a way and a time to introduce me to her. Grant me the grace to be responsive to all she has to offer me."

I had done so for months; perhaps this was to be an appointed test. Maybe this was the time and this was the day and the way for me to recognize her care and intercession for this seemingly impossible situation.

My illness persisted. Sure enough, I woke up on the morning of the Vigil with my other eye inflamed and pasted shut, with increased congestion, and with laryngitis added to the mix. I couldn't go to my Confirmation like this, I moaned; I looked awful and felt worse!

Our RCIA class was to rehearse at eight in the morning, and I dragged myself to church shivering in a cold drizzle of rain armed with cough lozenges, tissues, eye drops, and bottled water. I spotted Father Kelly and tearfully shared my anxiety and my fear that because of my aggravated health problems I wouldn't be able to be present that night. He quietly laid his hands on my head right in the middle of the aisle despite all the noise around us. He prayed for my healing and made the sign of the cross on my forehead. "Go in God's peace," he encouraged.

I spent a full and exciting but exhausting day with my four sons, all of whom were in town for my Confirmation, a rare occasion since two of them lived out of state. The sun was setting and no time remained even for a quick rest; weak as I felt, I only had time to dress and hurry to church—if I didn't collapse on the way.

I went ahead in faith, confident that God would somehow answer the many prayers on my behalf by all those intercessors whom I call my "Praying Eagles."

The drive to church takes twelve minutes. By the time I arrived and parked, my weakness had disappeared and—wonder of wonders—when I glanced in the mirror on my car visor, I looked normal! And I had recovered my speaking voice! Both of my eyes were clear and open. No one noticed or suspected that I had been so ill! God supplied more than enough strength for the prolonged sacred celebration of the evening, the Mass, and the lengthy reception for new members and friends afterward. I returned home after midnight full of amazement at the marvelous goodness of God and His obvious divine intervention.

I almost missed the wonderful day for which the Lord had destined me. *But God had His hand on my life!*

Our Almighty God and Father upheld me with His righteous right hand and His mighty arm! I suspect that the Virgin Mary might have had more than a little to do with it as she approached her Son on my behalf. Perhaps she simply stated my need to Him as she did at the wedding in Cana: "Son, Your child Leona is ill and has no strength." To God's ministering angels waiting to do Jesus' bidding, she might have turned and instructed, "Do whatever He tells you!" Jesus miraculously changed the common water of my mortal body's weakness into the new wine of His strength.

Afterglow

Our two RCIA leaders, looking handsome and dashing in their tuxedos, had given us an abundance of good insight in advance about what we might expect on that milestone night. However, I wasn't prepared for three startling things.

First, I couldn't wipe from my face the broad, joy-grin that persisted hours on end even after I turned off my bedroom light. Was it because I didn't want to wash off the holy anointing oil from my forehead? In the morning when I looked in the mirror, the joy-grin was still there! Like Moses' face that shone after he came down from his encounter with God on Mount Sinai, my joy-grin remained after the exquisite double blessing of receiving two sacraments in the same night—Confirmation, once for all—and the Eucharist—repeatable and spiritually nourishing for the rest of my life.

Second, no one told me that I would feel so spiritually "high" afterward that I thought my head was bouncing against the ceiling. Walking to my car in the church parking lot after the Vigil, I was afraid I would lift off like a helium balloon.

Third, no one told me that it was normal and to be expected that I would be sleepless on Easter Vigil night. Because I had been ill I was exhausted and looked forward to collapsing and dropping off immediately into sound, refreshing sleep. It was not to be! Hour after hour I tossed and turned and struggled to force sleep because I thought I needed it—but sleep eluded me. Grinning in the dark (perhaps glowing, too, I'm not sure!), I happily went over and over the wonderful events of this sacred night of nights. It was a big deal to me, especially at my advanced age, to embrace the fullness of faith in the Church which Christ Himself established and to be so warmly embraced by His people. I anticipated and was already experiencing an even deeper, more intimate, abiding relationship with Jesus Christ whom I had known and loved and served since my youth.

I finally crawled out of bed at dawn to face a rainy, fog-shrouded Easter Sunday morning with my eyes still wide open—I was surprised not to feel physically drained or mentally exhausted. After Easter Mass, my mentor, Rod, suggested that instead of wasting my time struggling to sleep, I should have gone with God's flow to stay awake in spiritual vigil all night—invest my time adoring the Lord, praying, meditating, praising, reading His Word and rejoicing in my wakefulness—offering it up as a sacrifice to Him.

Rod was a little late to tell me that in times past the Vigil celebration lasted until dawn in a symbolic, wakeful, watch night to re-present waiting for Jesus' resurrection on Easter morning.

Okay. Lord willing, I hope to be prepared for that next year at Easter Vigil. I wondered if my joy-grin and helium float feeling would last until then....

A Momentous Time

March 2005 was a month to be remembered for many reasons.

As significant as the time was for me personally, the Catholic world and the entire international community will never forget its historical importance. Everything seemed hushed as we lived quietly under the lengthening shadow of the final days of the illness and death of our beloved Pope John Paul II. The next weeks would hold both intense mourning and jubilant celebration on a scale heretofore unknown in world history. My Confirmation took place during the last days of the life of Pope John Paul II and within a few weeks of the election of Pope

Benedict XVI.

The above events were an end and a beginning, a termination and a commencement for the entire Catholic world. In a similar way, my Confirmation was that for me. I crossed a spiritual threshold into THE LAND OF MORE. Ahead of me lay MORE than I had experienced, a fullness of faith waiting to be savored. I crossed the Tiber River over the bridge of my Confirmation. I stepped into new territory; this was the Promised Land "flowing with milk and honey" that God had prepared for me.

Still MORE?

I honestly thought that my autobiography, *Czeching My Roots*, written as I approached my eighties, was the conclusion of my life story. I didn't anticipate any surprises. But God had much more in store. He launched me on an incredible new journey to the LAND OF MORE, the Catholic Church, which I have chronicled in this book. That new journey was an unexpected sequel or addendum to my life story.

Of course, there is still a sequel to that sequel! I am not finished; I am continuing the Christian faith journey which I began as an infant with the sacrament of my baptism. *God has kept His hand on my life* and continues to lead me further, deeper, closer, and higher!

I have leaped off the diving board into the deep waters of faith and spiritual experience in the Catholic Church. Now I am experiencing the joy and invigoration of learning to swim in its deep waters.

God is giving me the thrilling opportunity to explore THE LAND OF MORE, to mine its riches, enter into its mysteries, rejoice in its deeper biblical insights, bask in its sacred traditions, and share its treasures with others. And, if God wills, to write about some of those adventures as well!

My spiritual journey is ongoing and will not end until I am in the presence of our holy, mighty, immortal God and in the company of the Communion of Saints. With them I expect to keep singing the "Hallelujah Chorus" *ad majorem Dei gloriam,* to the greater glory of God throughout eternity.

OVER THE RIVER AND THROUGH THE WOODS

An Epilogue is defined as "a speech delivered by one of the actors at the end of a play." Since I am the actor whose surprising life drama God orchestrated in the pages of this book, I do have a few reflections upon completing my journey into THE LAND OF MORE, the Catholic Church.

My observations are, in another sense, like a Prologue, which is a "preface, introduction, beginning, a look ahead." I want to give the reader of my story an appetizing foretaste of the feast that lies ahead of one who takes that quantum leap over the river Tiber to begin the wonderful sacramental life of the Catholic Church.

I was eager to experience all the "goodies" I had heard about. I soon discovered that I would also have to go through the woods, or the desert, or the jungle on this continuing journey. I had to put on my pith helmet and trek off through the hassles and trials of everyday life carrying my cross even while enjoying the journey. It is true that there is a bountiful table spread in verdant pastures and beside restful waters (Psalm 23)—a picnic of sorts. But it is not entirely or always a picnic, and it often takes place in the wilderness. I shouldn't expect to wear the perpetual joy-grin and maintain the helium balloon emotional feelings that I initially experienced at my Confirmation. However, even the "dark night of the soul" and God-ordained times of adversity and trial are accompanied by treasures of darkness and deep blessings of progress in holiness as one moves toward maturity.

G.K. Chesterton observed that the Catholic Church is far larger and more wonderful inside than it appears from the outside. Prior to my Confirmation, I looked through a small keyhole in the door, so to speak. Now the door is flung open, and I am invited to walk in and make myself at home with all that implies. A life of delightful discovery, the unfolding of mysteries, and the unpacking of the fullness of the sacraments lie ahead of me. I can partake freely of the awesome and copious banquet of worship and adoration; I can taste and see the goodness of the Lord.

THE LAND OF MORE is a spiritually rich earthly vestibule to what Jesus called "My Father's House" where He went to prepare a place for us when He ascended into Heaven.

So what did I discover after I stepped over the threshold into the Church?

Mirrors and Wardrobes

I felt that I had come Home. Home implies family. Suddenly I have many new and former family relationships to sort out. How did God want me to relate to the wonderful evangelical family of faith from which I have come? Was I to isolate myself now and leave them behind? How should I successfully relate to my new Catholic family?

I was surprised to find what a greatly expanded Christian family I have now; it encompasses heaven and earth, past and present, people alive and those who have departed this earthly life. This was a new concept for me to understand and delight in.

I felt like the fictional character, Alice, who passed through the looking glass into Wonderland, a fantasy place of strange animals and peculiar people. Or like the curious children who stepped through the wardrobe to explore the imaginary land of Narnia. The Catholic LAND OF MORE beckoned as a multi-faceted safari and I was the eager explorer.

I wrestled long and hard with theology and doctrine and tried my best not to be drawn into the Catholic Church. My journey Home was primarily an intellectual journey of reason to find the Truth. When I was ultimately convinced that the Truth did lie in the Church, I couldn't resist it; it was all very heady. But as soon as the gift of faith took over, my heart and emotions became joyously involved.

Now, however, flesh and blood encounters with people in the Catholic Church were something else! It had been easier to deal with dogma!

Suddenly the very people I had previously avoided and criticized were my family, my brothers and sisters in Christ. They had not changed; I had changed in my perception of them. They had nothing to say about my being dropped into their midst. As "the new kid on the block" I was one of the formerly "separated brethren." I was among them for better or worse and not only "until death would us part." We were together for eternity! However, I wondered if they would accept me in real time on earth. Would I ever have as close bonds with them as I had with my evangelical friends?

"I Do" Led Me Here

Shortly after I married my husband more than sixty years ago, we sailed off literally "on a slow boat to China." I was going to my bridegroom's home which was to become my home. Upon our arrival in Hong Kong, a happy crowd of nearly a hundred members of his extended family nearly smothered us with their boisterous welcome. They waited eagerly on the dock for the first glimpse of Ted's new American wife. Their expectations of me ran high.

Instantly I had nine brothers- and sisters-in-law, their spouses and children, innumerable in-law nieces and nephews, aunts and uncles, cousins, and a sizable contingent of shirttail relatives who didn't want to miss the action. At the top of the list were new authority figures—a mother-in-law and father-in-law whom I was to honor.

Initially, I couldn't communicate; I had to learn a new language. I was immediately immersed in ethnic and family and cultural traditions which I would be expected to embrace because of my new role as my husband's wife. To say that this Iowa-born girl was in culture shock is to put it mildly.

I experienced living in a sweltering tropical climate for the first time. I had to become accustomed to strange new foods. I struggled to observe new protocol among the family—to address relatives by titles according to their birth order! There were new festivals and events and national heroes to celebrate, even a different calendar based on phases of the moon. It was not the current year by the A.D. or C.E. count, but the year four-thousand-something. Their music sounded strange and dissonant to my American ears. A British system of government had jurisdiction over me now. When I went through immigration upon arrival, an official issued me a new identity card. Hong Kong was a British crown colony back then, and residents were called subjects, not citizens. They owed allegiance to a queen and a kingdom far away which most of them had never seen.

Nevertheless, this was my permanent new home. I said "I do" at my wedding, and there was no turning back. I was happily committed; I needed and wanted to be accepted. I had to be humble; I was not there to impress the established family of my spouse but to find my place in it. I was there to learn. Success would require much time and loving patience on both sides.

A Stone Seeking Its Place

When I was received into the Catholic Church, it was like encountering a new culture with all the above ramifications and culture shock.

I anticipated making cross-cultural adjustments when we engaged in our missionary work overseas. As a Catholic convert now, I too am confronted with a different language; I must learn *Catholic-speak!* I have the same Bible, and my belief is still "one Lord, one faith, one baptism, one God and Father of all…" (Ephesians 4:4-5). However, even common theological terms and Bible expressions have expanded shades of meaning. There are new customs, traditions, disciplines, feast days, celebrations, and solemnities to observe. Catholic Christians have different worship attitudes and habits, devotional expressions and practices, literature, music, and social interactions, although we love and serve the same Lord Jesus Christ.

Understanding My New Family

The Catholic family of faith has many faces. It is a blend of various cultures and ethnic backgrounds because the Catholic Church is *catholic*—universal, worldwide, and international. As a newcomer, I need to walk softly to become assimilated into this established family. I am a new stone approaching an existing, ancient, time-honored spiritual building that is both invisible and visible. It takes time for a previously out-of-place-stone to be "fitly joined together." I am sure to need quite a bit of chiseling and chipping and polishing along with the oil of the Holy Spirit before I become a smooth fit.

When approaching my new Catholic family, I didn't want to give the impression of pride regardless of how well known I might have been in my evangelical context. I shouldn't assume an attitude of "Hey, look me over. Aren't you lucky to have me in the Catholic Church?" *Wrong!*

In Hong Kong, a driver under instruction must affix a large letter "L" for *Learner* to the bumper of his car to notify other drivers and pedestrians of his beginner status. To express a genuine *Learner* attitude suits the new convert far better: "Hi. I'm a new Catholic. I have a lot to learn, and I hope you might help me." *Yes!*

My friends warned me that Catholics would not be as "warm and fuzzy" as evangelicals, so I shouldn't expect spontaneous hugs or to be given a lively welcome party. This proved only partially true; in due course I was surprised, in fact almost overwhelmed, by their warmth and loving acceptance. It is worth the patient wait because new friendships take time to take root and flourish.

By and large, Catholics are homegrown in their parishes. They are not as mobile and church-hopping as evangelicals. The wonderful legacy of many faithful Catholic families is that their children come up the ladder from Baptism as infants through Catholic school, Confirmation, marriage, and beyond. Most have long ago established their affinity groups and are comfortable in their own circles where people know each other well. I must understand that as a convert I am starting out as an outsider.

Dealing with "Friendly Fire"

Whenever I begin to take any deeper spiritual step, I can count on the spiritual adversary to be right on my tail; he didn't let up on me when I settled into THE LAND OF MORE. I recognize this struggle for what it is—spiritual warfare. Misunderstanding and criticism from my evangelical friends to my becoming Catholic certainly didn't stop with my Confirmation. Rather than complain about it or try to avoid unpleasant encounters, I'm learning that it is better to welcome such potential conflicts as continuing opportunities for gentle apologetics—reasoned and loving witness and defense of God's full truth.

As I explore the riches of THE LAND OF MORE, it becomes clearer that God is calling me to "spiritual bridgework." I am delighted to go back and forth on the bridge over the Tiber. I don't do so in retreat or vacillation but in order to meet friends and strangers on the bridge and invite them over to THE LAND OF MORE. What joy to lead them by the hand and by the heart to the fullness of the Christian faith I have found! I can share with them biblical answers to their questions, clear up misunderstandings, dispel prejudices, and pray for their personal needs. The point is not to win arguments or have knock-down, drag-out doctrinal debates. My evangelical Christian friends are not "enemy combatants." I hope to engage them with mutual respect and genuine love, with the wisdom of the Holy Spirit and covered by much prayer. I understand where they are coming from because I walked in their shoes for many long years.

What Is This "Fullness"?

Do I consider what I believed previously as an evangelical Christian to be invalid or wide of the mark? No, I sincerely appreciate my strong evangelical background and biblical training. Nevertheless, I believe it to have been incomplete. The biblical foundation is the same, but in the Catholic Church there is MORE of what God revealed. It is not added on; it has been there from the beginning and was passed on from the time of Jesus and through His apostles. There is fullness that I have still barely tapped into in the comparatively short time since I stepped over the threshold. There are many wonderful spiritual truths and interpretations of Scripture that are blossoming before my very eyes and in my thirsty spirit. I stand on tiptoe of expectancy as I keep unpacking the rich spiritual treasures in the Church that Christ established.

At the same time, I don't wear rose-colored glasses. In the Apostles' Creed I affirm that I believe in "the holy catholic church." I am not so naïve as to expect that the earthly expression of the Church is already perfect. Yes, the Church is one (Ephesians 4:3-6), but practical unity is still being worked out in order to become what Jesus prayed for in John 17:17-23. The Church as the Body of Christ *is holy* because God is holy and Jesus as its Head is holy; it is not a product of good ideas or the invention of men who exercise private interpretation. The Church as it exists on earth is made up of imperfect and not-yet-holy people in the pews and in leadership. All followers of Jesus are human and all are in the process of working out their own salvation and unity and holiness as the Apostle Paul exhorted us to do in Philippians 2:12-13. Nevertheless, there is immense richness and fullness in God's revelation that we can experience in the visible Church on Earth.

There are spiritual riches in its liturgical worship that I have only begun to understand and appreciate. This wealth involves my senses, which are good because God created them. There is richness in the Church's sacraments, in adoration, silent contemplation, meditation, pilgrimages, and sacramentals. The beauty of its art, architecture, basilicas, shrines, and cathedrals is unsurpassed. I am discovering poetry, drama, history, literature, and music I never delved into previously. The esthetic table is lavishly and generously spread before me. Besides nurturing some of the humblest, truly saintly people whom the world has ever known, the Catholic Church has produced some of the greatest intellectual giants who have contributed to every field of knowledge through the centuries.

Fleshing Out the "MORES"

I anticipate discovering MORE and MORE of the treasure of the Catholic Church as time goes on. The following are only a few choice gems among many:

There are MORE biblical ramifications to what Jesus meant when He declared "I will build my Church" than I previously understood.

The Eucharist is far MORE than mere symbolism; it is the real Presence of Jesus in the transubstantiation of the elements (John 6). When I receive His body and blood MORE often, I am infused with His supernatural power and built up in my spirit.

MORE intercessors are available to help in my needs and to obtain help for others by enlisting the prayers of the living saints in heaven.

MORE than that, I can freely avail myself of the uniquely powerful intercession of Jesus' Mother.

I have MORE brothers and sisters in Christ living on earth and in heaven than I ever imagined when I previously excluded parts of His Body by my narrow doctrinal interpretations.

Through Sacred Tradition and the Early Church Fathers, we have MORE knowledge and understanding of the direct teachings of Jesus and His apostles, none of which contradict the Bible; rather, they amplify and apply God's revelation.

There is MORE reliable God-ordained authority in the Pope and the Magisterium to preserve and protect the revealed truth of God, to interpret the Word of God, and to guide and nurture my spiritual life than in my finite private interpretation.

Through God's loving provision of Purgatory for the forgiven Christian's purification process, I have MORE opportunity for final sanctification and holiness to prepare for my entrance to heaven.

I have MORE assurance of forgiveness by availing myself of the way which Jesus provided and prescribed—through the absolution of my confessed sins by a priest who is ordained and authorized to do so *in persona Christi* (Matt. 18:18; John 20: 22-23; James 5:13-15).

Through taking advantage of the sacraments of the Church I can receive MORE graces to continuously build up my Christian faith and life.

In the liturgy of the Church I tap into MORE of the magnificence of our biblical and spiritual heritage than by preaching alone.

I have access to MORE solidly biblical spiritual literature by holy men and women of God, past and present, than I ever knew existed.

I have MORE opportunity for divine healing through the sacraments and prayer, specifically through partaking of the

Eucharist and the anointing of the sick.

I have MORE biblical understanding of the place of redemptive suffering in the life of a Christian and a deeper perception of carrying one's cross.

I have MORE opportunity to receive and exercise the gifts of the Spirit within the visible Church for the building up of its members and under its protective accountability than to exercise them as a "lone ranger."

I hear MORE Scripture read during the Liturgy of the Word in every Mass from all parts of the Bible in balance, by scriptural themes, and simultaneously throughout the world and all through the Church calendar year than in sermon-centered churches.

There is MORE opportunity to adore and contemplate our Lord Jesus Christ even outside the timetable of the Mass through the exposition of the Blessed Sacrament.

I have a MORE biblical understanding of the "we" of the Church, the entire Body of Christ, the "our Father" in community and communion in contrast to an exclusive emphasis on "me" and "my personal Savior."

There is MORE to the authentic biblical gospel than verbalizing a once-for-all brief prayer to accept Jesus as one's personal Savior, however sincere, and expecting to receive an instant guarantee of heaven.

God will judge us on MORE than the verbal confession of our faith. At His final judgment He will look for and base it on the demonstration of our faith by our works (Matthew 25:31-46; James 2:13-26).

There is MORE emphasis in the Scriptures on working out our own salvation (never working *for* salvation), proving our faith by our fruits and good works, the necessity of remaining in

Christ, and enduring faithfully to the end than taking isolated texts out of context in an attempt to prove "once saved, always saved."

Baptism is far MORE than an optional outward symbol; it is an essential, initial sacrament that effects what it signifies. "By water and the spirit" (John 3: 3,5) a person is cleansed from original sin, is born again, is placed "in Christ," becomes indwelt by the Holy Spirit, rejects Satan and all evil, accepts the Lordship of Christ, and becomes a part of Jesus' Church.

There is MORE biblical basis for infant baptism than there is for the dedication of a child or a christening ritual. The Sacrament of Baptism brings about on behalf of the child the above graces through the assent of the parents, the action and words of the priest, the witness of family and godparents and the congregation, and the element of water.

WELCOME TO THE FULLNESS OF *THE LAND OF MORE!*